# bake until golden brown

## *Britney* BREAKS BREAD

BRITNEY BROWN-CHAMBERLAIN

# 83 press®

Copyright © 2024 by 83 Press

All rights reserved. No part of this book may be reproduced or transmitted in any form or by any means, electronic or mechanical, including photocopying, or by any information storage and retrieval system, without permission in writing from 83 Press. Reviewers may quote brief passages for specific inclusion in a magazine or newspaper.

83 Press
2323 2nd Avenue North
Birmingham, Alabama 35203
83press.com

ISBN: 979-8-9899185-0-8
Printed in China

DEDICATION

To my dear husband, whose unwavering support and encouragement have fueled my culinary passion: thank you for being my rock and my greatest taste-tester. I dedicate these recipes to you, my forever sous chef and partner in all things sweet and savory. I love you with all that I am.

To my precious children, whose giggles echo through our kitchen and whose eager hands help me mix, measure, and bake: this cookbook is a labor of love dedicated to you, who make every moment in the kitchen an adventure filled with laughter and learning. May these recipes become cherished memories shared around our family table and may they inspire you to explore the world of cooking with the same enthusiasm and joy that you bring to our home every day.

To my dearest grandmother, whose kitchen was always filled with my favorite treats, from butter-laden Cream of Wheat to frozen sugared grapes to the most decadent holiday spreads: this cookbook is a tribute to the boundless love you infused into every dish and the countless hours we've spent together in the kitchen. These memories flavor every dish that I create.

To my cherished Nanny, whose adventurous spirit and unwavering encouragement guided me through a world of new foods and flavors: your gentle nudges to explore beyond the familiar paved the way for my culinary journey, and I dedicate these recipes to you, my forever inspiration in the kitchen. Thank you for widening my global perspective through food, travel, literature, and music. Words cannot express the gratitude I have for you.

To my incredible parents and baby sister, Bobbie, (yes, you'll always be my baby!): Where do I even begin? Mom and Dad, you gave Bobbie and me the best childhood, and this cookbook is a testament to your belief in my creative expression. You always allowed me to explore whatever flight of fancy that blew my way, my whacky whimsical ideas, and gave me the platform to feel that I could truly be whatever I wanted to be. I dedicate these recipes to the three of you, my guiding lights, whose love has nurtured not only my culinary passion but also my adventurous spirit. May these dishes make you proud and bring you as much joy and fulfillment as you have brought me throughout the years. Thank you for believing in me. You guys rock.

## contents

| | | |
|---|---|---|
| | 14 | baking basics |
| 4 dedication | 26 | my 5 must-have recipes |
| 8 acknowledgements | 32 | a morning pick-me-up |
| 10 introduction | 62 | fruity and fabulous |

| 92  | a little something savory |     |                 |
|-----|---------------------------|-----|-----------------|
| 114 | nutty necessities         | 192 | autumn delights |
| 138 | from the garden           | 224 | chocolate heaven |
| 160 | family favorites          | 254 | recipe index    |

ACKNOWLEDGMENTS

*Thank you.* Two simple words, yet they hold the weight of my deepest appreciation and heartfelt joy. Writing a cookbook is never a solitary endeavor, and this book is as much yours as it is mine.

As I sit down to write this, I find myself overwhelmed with gratitude for your decision to bring my cookbook into your kitchen. I poured my heart and soul into crafting each recipe, infusing them with love, passion, and a sprinkle of magic. And now, as they find their way into your hands and onto your countertops, I can't help but feel a profound sense of connection—a shared love for the simple joys of homemade treats and the moments of togetherness they create.

As you dive into the recipes within these pages, may you find joy in every whisk, satisfaction in every bite, and a sense of accomplishment in every creation. And remember, behind each recipe is my heartfelt thanks to you for choosing to embark on this delicious journey with me.

Your support means more to me than words can express.

*xoxo,*

*Britney*

INTRODUCTION

# step into my kitchen

I truly believe that everything happens for a reason. I'm also a firm believer that if you want to make God laugh, tell him your plans.

I would love to say that I went to pastry school, studied at Le Cordon Bleu, opened my own cottage bakery, and the rest was history. However, that couldn't be further from the truth. The truth is that I'm a science nerd who set out to study medicine and become a plastic surgeon. I wanted to help people feel better about themselves.

I went to Penn State, studied hard, and out of the blue realized that maybe this wasn't the path for me. So, I went into cancer research at Drexel University, got my master's degree, and just knew that I'd be moving up the corporate ladder. Then, the COVID-19 pandemic hit. Before we get into that, let's rewind a bit—I'm skipping over A LOT.

In addition to being a science nerd, I was also a band geek. I've always been a free spirit. I was the kid who would go outside, dig a hole in the ground, fill it with water, and literally cover myself in mud. I would play with worms and creepy crawlers, and I loved exploring.

On rainy days when I couldn't go outside, I'd be in the kitchen, mixing things together and plopping them in the oven just to see what would happen. I was conducting my very first science experiments. When I was about 8 or 9, my mom bought my sister and me a Betty Crocker Bake'n Fill Cake Mold, and I never looked back! I'd pack that pan with chocolate and peanut butter and jelly and anything my little brain could conjure up just to see what happened when it baked up in the oven.

Needless to say, there were MANY disasters. But also, many successes.

I come from a family of serious cooks. I'm talking throw-down, eat until your eyes pop out and your pants no longer fit. I can still smell the scent of my mom's cooking waking me up on Thanksgiving morning. I have so many fond food memories, but most importantly, my food memories always involve love.

During my college years, I didn't cook much. Then, in 2014, I met my husband. Our first date was at a Chinese-French fusion restaurant, and

I had just landed the job of my dreams and began working from home. The crazy part is, I thought that working from home would be amazing with all the freedom it allowed me, but it was just more alienating. I started to cook even more. Wanting that connection I was missing with my family and work life, I started posting my recipes and concoctions on my Instagram.

When I tell you folks were messaging me daily for recipes, I started to think to myself, "Maybe I should start a blog." But I am not tech savvy. I didn't even know how to work a camera, much less write a recipe where people could go and bake my creations in their own kitchen. Then, on a cool fall night, I was on the couch when "Britney Breaks Bread" popped into my head, and I just thought that it was too cool a name not to at least see what could happen.

It was the best decision ever. I remember waking up the next day with 11 followers and thinking, "Whoa! Eleven people want to see me cook?" I cooked more and more and then I got hooked! Every day, I was teaching and challenging myself to make things I'd never made before.

When I finally mastered the elusive puff pastry, it was on. I got a real kick out of taking simple things like butter, flour, and sugar and making something absolutely delicious. I made more cakes than I could eat and more bread than anyone could ever fathom consuming.

The more I baked, the more I wanted to. I was bitten by the bug! When I became confident

he ate everything. And so did I! I thought to myself, "This could be something serious." Our love grew as we got to know each other through food. On one of our dates, this man made me a filet mignon, asparagus, and roasted potatoes, and it was cooked to perfection. It was history from there. We traveled the world and would often try to make many of the foods that we'd eaten abroad at home. For the most part, he did all the cooking. And me? I did most of the eating.

We moved together to Maryland, about three hours away from my family. Initially, I was quite homesick. After growing up with my cousins and aunts and uncles all within a 5- to 30-minute drive, it was weird not having them around. In true "me" fashion, I began to try to re-create a bit of home in my own kitchen. More importantly, I didn't want him out-cooking me, so I started cooking again.

enough, I began to write down my recipes and explore flavors and post them to my website, *britneybreaksbread.com*.

Fast-forward some years, *Britney Breaks Bread* has more than 500 recipes full of quick weeknight meals, tons of decadent baked treats, and holiday recipes that will make you the talk of the town, and now, I'm writing an actual cookbook, which, as I write these words, is still so incredibly surreal.

*Bake Until Golden Brown* is not just a cookbook about food. Yes, it's mostly about food, but each recipe is so personal and has so much meaning to me. I started writing this book when I was 38 weeks pregnant, which was such a pivotal and beautiful time in my life. Several times when I was recipe-testing, my brand-new baby girl was asleep on my chest as I danced around the kitchen trying to quietly knead dough and whisk together eggs and sugar.

My husband, toddler, and neighbors have all been my taste-testers. My parents even drove down for a food party! So, this book is deeper than food. It's literally a piece of me and my loved ones in every single ingredient, step, photo, and recommendation.

It is my dream that, like me, you fall in love with baking, enjoy the feeling of flour on your hands and every sneaked spoonful of cake batter (even though you're not supposed to eat it), and are always excited to bake forth the deliciousness your oven can bring.

Whether you're looking for a showstopping dessert or a yummy cake recipe to enjoy while snuggled up on the couch, may you always refer to this book for a piece of happiness, hope, and love.

xoxo,
*Britney*

# baking basics

# understanding the magic of baking

I never set out to become a baker. In fact, I spent the better part of my 20s avoiding the kitchen altogether. But life, with its peculiar twists and unexpected detours, often has a way of leading us to our true passions.

One sunny fall afternoon, I was craving pumpkin bread and found a random recipe on the internet. After about 20 minutes of prep, flour dusted my cheeks and melted butter coated my apron, but the aroma of spice began to fill my tiny apartment. It was intoxicating. When I finally pulled the loaf pan from the oven, I stared in disbelief at the tragedy that was this bread. It was flat, dry, and somehow had no flavor even though my entire apartment smelled like Bath and Body Works on the first of September.

Frustrated with the outcome, I began reworking the recipe. Why was it flat? Was it the leavening? The melted butter? Why didn't it taste good even though it smelled heavenly? Did it need more salt? More spices? Why was it dry? Did it need more butter or oil? More milk? Buttermilk? Sour cream?

This experience is when I first fell in love with baking. Ever since, I have been experimenting in the kitchen. My entire baking journey has been one science experiment, and I get such a thrill. Each success fuels my excitement, and each failure teaches me something new.

I want to share what I've learned and what makes a successful bake every single time. I remember how intimidating those first steps can be. Let me be your guide! I want this book to be a companion for each aspiring baker, a testament to the magic that happens when flour meets water, and a reminder that even the most seasoned bakers were once beginners.

From butter to baking soda, here is a breakdown of my baking basics; keep them in your back pocket to make you an even better home baker.

For the purposes of this book and most baking recipes, wheat flour can be divided into three main areas: all-purpose, bread, and cake flour. Luckily, they gave the flour types pretty easy names to remember their uses. While all are made from the same stuff (wheat), the flours' differences come down to protein, specifically gluten.

### ALL-PURPOSE FLOUR

If you're only going to have one bag of flour in your pantry, it's likely going to be all-purpose flour. It's made from a blend of soft and hard wheat for a consistency that's coarser than cake flour but finer than bread flour, and the protein content can range anywhere from 10% to 12%. I bake a ton with all-purpose; it's the universal flour for a reason. If a recipe calls for cake flour and you don't have any, you can use all-purpose flour in its place. All-purpose provides a balance of both structure and tenderness, making it the most versatile flour, fit for all types of baked goods.

### BREAD FLOUR

When we're making a yeasted bread, the more gluten, the better, which is why you want a higher-protein flour (i.e., bread flour). It's milled from hard wheat, which gives it a slightly coarser texture. Bread flour has about 12% to 14% protein, which yields high gluten formation and gives bread dough its gorgeous, elastic texture that leads to a beautiful, chewy final product. This is ideal for not only loaves of bread but also bagels, pizza crust, certain types of cookies, and even some pastries (like cinnamon rolls).

### CAKE FLOUR

For a soft, delicate cake, you want something with a low protein level (i.e., cake flour). The protein content of cake flour is about 6% to 8%, and it's made from soft wheat, giving it a smoother, finer texture. This type of flour doesn't develop gluten as much as a bread or all-purpose flour, so it results in a more tender, delicate crumb, which is exactly what you want for a cake. Cake flour can also be used for biscuits, cupcakes, cookies, pancakes, muffins, and doughnuts.

---

As you grow more comfortable with baking, you can experiment with switching out flours and see how the results vary. Let's say you have a chocolate chip cookie recipe that calls for all-purpose flour (like my Classic Chocolate Chip Cookies on page 226). You love the recipe, but you want it to be a little chewier. Try swapping in bread flour. If you're making a cake with all-purpose flour, try making it with cake flour for a softer crumb. The results are truly tangible—you can literally feel the difference when you bite into it.

# sugar

Life's better with a little sweetness! I love sugar so much; not only does it sweeten things up but it also is so important to the final texture of your baked goods. Sugar interferes with the formation of gluten by competing with flour for water. It's both hydrophilic and hygroscopic, which simply means that it attracts and holds moisture. This results in a more tender crumb. In meringues, sugar is a stabilizer, and in recipes that call for yeast (like breads), sugar helps the yeast produce carbon dioxide, which helps the dough rise.

### GRANULATED & BROWN SUGAR

There are two main types of sugar, granulated (or white) and brown sugar, and their main difference all comes down to one key ingredient: molasses. Brown sugar is just granulated sugar that has molasses mixed in, and dark brown sugar has more molasses than light brown sugar does. That also means you can make your own brown sugar at home if you ever run out, as long as you always keep granulated sugar and molasses on hand. Simply add 1 tablespoon (21 grams) molasses to 1 cup (200 grams) granulated sugar and stir.

Brown sugar has a softer texture, and it helps give your baked goods a deeper flavor (because of the molasses). Just remember that molasses is acidic, so if a recipe calls for light brown sugar, don't just swap it for dark brown! Dark brown sugar has nearly double the molasses as light, and it can impact the desired texture of the final baked good if it's not the intended sugar for use. Of note, all my recipes call for light brown sugar, so no worries on running to the store for dark brown.

### CONFECTIONERS' SUGAR

Then there's confectioners' sugar, sometimes called powdered sugar, which is simply sugar and cornstarch. (You can also make this at home in a pinch.) Confectioners' sugar acts as a stabilizer and sweetener for buttercreams, glazes, meringues, whipped creams, and more. It's also pretty when dusted on top of baked goods as a garnish, like in my Cherry-Almond Cake (see page 120). I also use confectioners' sugar in my no-bake cheesecakes (like my No-Bake Sweet Potato Cheesecake on page 221) because it thickens the filling and allows it to set.

### HONEY

Lastly, there's honey! Well, this isn't the last for sure, because there's also maple syrup and coconut sugar and so on. However, for the purposes of this book, we have to discuss honey because I love it, and it's nature's gift to us! Like sugar, honey is also hygroscopic, but it adds a unique flavor that's like a fragrant cross between caramel and butterscotch, but has its own *je ne sais quoi*.

In some recipes, honey can function as a binder (think granola bars), and in others, it helps to caramelize baked goods in the oven. But don't swap out sugar for honey without adjusting the recipe! Honey is slightly acidic, which can affect the pH balance of your batter or dough. This can influence the texture and rise of the final product. To account for this, you might need to adjust the amount of baking soda to neutralize the acidity from the added honey. I like to use ½ cup (170 grams) honey per 1 cup (200 grams) of granulated sugar plus a pinch of baking soda.

# salt

In a health-conscious world, a lot of people are afraid of salt, but—news flash—you need it! When used correctly, salt enhances the flavors of other ingredients in the dish. Think of salt as that one friend whom everyone loves. They might not be the star of the show, but when they're not around, you desperately wish they were.

Growing up, salt was salt. As I started following online recipes and developing my own, I realized not all salt is created equal. "Table" salt is great for when you're seasoning savory recipes to taste, but I develop all my baking recipes with kosher salt. In fact, I don't use table salt AT ALL. Once I discovered kosher salt, it was a wrap. Kosher salt is just straight salt without the iodine additives you usually find in table salt. It will give you a purer "salt" flavor. Don't believe me? Try it for yourself. Try a pinch of table salt and then a pinch of kosher salt. You'll notice a difference in flavor from the anticaking agents and additives in the table salt.

That being said, can you simply sub one for the other? No! The size and shape of crystals in table salt and kosher salt are vastly different. I actually don't recommend using table salt at all for any of my recipes; this holds true for both the recipes in my cookbook and the recipes on my blog. However, if you must, know that table salt is much finer. If a recipe calls for 1 tablespoon (9 grams) kosher salt and you use 1 tablespoon (18 grams) table salt, you'll find your recipe will be way too salty. Simply decrease the volume of kosher salt called for in the recipe by half to get the weight of table salt.

## fats

There's one thing I know for certain: fat equals flavor every single time. Fat carries flavor; fat enhances flavor; you need fats. They also provide moisture. Remember how there's gluten in flour? Gluten develops as flour absorbs water, and that beautiful fat helps block that absorption, allowing for less gluten development and a more tender final product. That's why in a lot of basic bread recipes, you don't often add fat to the dough, because you want as much water absorbed as possible to help the gluten develop. In comparison, you can add a variety of different fats (sour cream, butter, oil, shortening, etc.) to a cake recipe to help reduce the amount of water being absorbed by the flour, resulting in a tender cake.

There are many kinds of fats, but the main sources of fats are butter (my favorite), oil, and shortening. When you think of butter, think of flavor! The average stick of butter sits at about 80% fat to 20% water in volume. (European butter has a bit higher butterfat percentage). In comparison, shortening is 100% hydrogenated oil with no additional water. Because of this, shortening often results in lighter, airier baked goods (just without the added flavor of butter). So, what do I do? I like to mix them for both fluffy texture and added flavor.

### BUTTER

Butter is a cornerstone ingredient in baking, profoundly influencing both the flavor and texture of baked goods. Its rich, creamy taste is unparalleled, imparting a depth of flavor that is both luxurious and comforting. When used in recipes such as cookies, cakes, and pastries, butter enhances the overall flavor profile, adding a subtle sweetness and a pleasant mouthfeel. The fat content in butter also carries and intensifies other flavors, ensuring that each bite is uniformly delicious.

In addition to its flavor-enhancing properties, butter plays a critical role in the texture and structure of baked goods. When creamed with sugar, butter helps incorporate air into the batter, creating a light and fluffy texture essential for cakes and certain cookies. Its high-fat content contributes to a tender crumb and a moist, soft interior in cakes and muffins. In pastry-making, cold butter creates flaky layers as it melts during baking, producing the characteristic flakiness of items like croissants, piecrusts, and puff pastry. Moreover, butter's ability to solidify at lower temperatures helps baked goods maintain their shape and structure, ensuring a perfect rise and a delightful texture.

### SHORTENING

Shortening is a vital ingredient in baking, primarily known for its ability to create exceptionally tender and flaky textures. Made from vegetable oils that are hydrogenated to become solid at room temperature, shortening lacks the water content found in butter. This absence of water prevents the formation of gluten, which in turn results in a more tender crumb in baked goods. In piecrusts and pastries, shortening's high melting point allows it to remain solid longer during the baking process, helping create the distinct flaky layers that are highly prized in these types of baked goods.

Moreover, shortening contributes to the stability and consistency of baked goods. Unlike butter, which has a lower melting point and can cause cookies to spread too much or cakes to lose their structure, shortening maintains its shape well when heated. This property makes it ideal for recipes that require precise shapes and textures, such as sugar cookies and certain types of bread. Additionally, shortening's neutral flavor allows the other ingredients' tastes to shine through without being overshadowed, making it a versatile fat choice for various baked goods. Its ability to stay stable at room temperature also contributes to a longer shelf life for finished products.

## OILS

Oils play a crucial role in baking, primarily influencing the texture and moisture of baked goods. Unlike solid fats such as butter and shortening, oils are liquid at room temperature, which helps create a different texture profile. When used in cakes, muffins, and quick breads, oils contribute to a moist, tender crumb that remains soft even after several days. This is because oils coat the flour proteins more completely than solid fats, preventing excessive gluten formation and ensuring a tender result. Additionally, oils can enhance the overall richness of the baked product without imparting any additional flavors, especially when using neutral oils like vegetable or canola oil.

Beyond moisture and tenderness, oils can also contribute to the longevity and consistency of baked goods. Baked goods made with oil tend to have a longer shelf life because oil does not solidify or crystallize at cooler temperatures, keeping the texture soft and palatable. Furthermore, oils are particularly useful in recipes where a consistent texture is desired, such as in brownies or dense cakes, as they provide uniform fat distribution. Some oils, like olive or coconut oil, can also impart unique flavors that enhance the overall taste of the baked goods, adding a layer of rich complexity.

## SOUR CREAM

Sour cream is the ingredient that was voted most likely to succeed in high school because it does all the things that we love. It's a versatile ingredient in baking, significantly enhancing the texture, moisture, and flavor of baked goods. Sour cream is one of those ingredients that I always use when I want something that's flavorful and moist (like my Aunt Hazel's Citrus Pound Cake on page 165). Its high fat content contributes to a tender and moist crumb, which is particularly beneficial in cakes, muffins, and quick breads. The fat helps create a rich, luxurious texture while preventing the gluten from over-developing, ensuring the final product is soft and tender. Additionally, the moisture in sour cream keeps baked goods from drying out, extending their shelf life and maintaining their freshness over time. (Bonus points for sour cream!)

Beyond its textural benefits, sour cream also adds a subtle tangy flavor that can elevate the overall taste of baked goods. The acidity in sour cream reacts with baking soda, producing carbon dioxide gas that helps the dough or batter rise. This chemical reaction can result in a lighter, fluffier texture, particularly in recipes that rely on leavening agents (which we'll talk about next). Furthermore, the acidity can help balance the sweetness of the baked goods, adding complexity and depth to the flavor profile. When used in cakes, cookies, or even some savory recipes, sour cream can enhance both the texture and taste.

# leavening agents

Have you ever been really excited about a cake, but you weren't measuring that closely and it came out a little soapy? More than likely, you added too much baking soda. Baking soda is classified as a "chemical" leavening agent. It's how muffins rise tall and cakes double in size.

To take you back to science class for a second, do you remember the pH scale? With acids and bases? Well, baking soda is a base. When you mix it with an acid (like vinegar, lemon juice, or buttermilk), it will react, bubbling up. Each bubble contains carbon dioxide, which is really what is making your muffins rise and your cakes double. As you tear into a baked good, you can see the result of this reaction in the tiny little pockets where that carbon dioxide once existed.

In a way, you can also taste the reaction. When you mix a base and an acid, you're left with two things: carbon dioxide (the bubbles) and salt. In a lot of recipes that call for just baking powder, you'll see only a little bit of salt in the ingredient list. You can easily over-salt a baked good if you're not careful.

All that being said, a little baking soda goes a long way. You only need about ¼ teaspoon (1.25 grams) per 1 cup (125 grams) flour! If you add too much, you get that soapy taste I mentioned earlier because it won't fully activate. Similarly, if you don't have something like lemon juice or buttermilk to activate your baking soda and make it bubble, you'll end up with that taste again because nothing is activating the baking soda.

Because not every recipe calls for a prominent acid, you have the wonder that is baking powder. It gives you the best of both worlds by combining baking soda with a low-level acid (usually cream of tartar). But if they're already combined, how do the bubbles happen? I'm glad you asked. In most cases, baking powder is double-acting. It needs liquid and heat. When you add it to your wet ingredients, it'll have its first reaction, and it'll have its second reaction as it bakes in the oven. That's why it's important to bake items with baking powder right away for the best results.

# emulsions & extracts

Hear me out. Most people are familiar with extracts. You probably have a bottle of vanilla extract in your kitchen cabinet as you read this. You might even have almond or lemon extract if you do a lot of baking. Extracts provide a concentrated punch of flavor that helps enhance and refine the taste of your baked goods. I love to layer them on top of natural ingredients for an even more intense flavor profile.

Extracts are great, but emulsions? Emulsions are where it is AT. If extracts are diamonds, emulsions are emeralds and rubies. A lot of people, including seasoned bakers, might not be as familiar with emulsions, but I love them.

I stumbled upon them at my local specialty baking shop and did some research on them, gave them a chance, and haven't looked back since. They are such a great investment in your pantry and may be a bit pricey, but let me tell you, they are so worth it.

Extracts are alcohol-based, which means they will bake out in the oven. Emulsions are water-soluble, so they stick around even in high heat. More importantly, they result in a purer, stronger flavor by the end of baking. While emulsions are not necessary for you to enjoy my baking (in fact, they're optional!), I strongly urge you to go out and get one to try out. I promise you'll love it.

BAKING BASICS

# my 5 must-have recipes

*All the best bakers have a handful of recipes they revisit over and over again. These are my five staples that I use throughout this book. As you grow as a baker, take these recipes with you and customize them to the flavors you love. I can't wait to see what you create!*

# swiss meringue buttercream
### MAKES ABOUT 5 CUPS

- 1 tablespoon (15 grams) fresh lemon juice
- 6 large egg whites (180 grams)
- 1¾ cups (350 grams) granulated sugar
- 2 cups (454 grams) unsalted butter, room temperature
- ½ cup (60 grams) confectioners' sugar
- 1 teaspoon (6 grams) vanilla bean paste
- ¼ teaspoon kosher salt

**1.** In the bowl of a stand mixer, place lemon juice. Using a paper towel, wipe down sides and bottom of bowl with lemon juice until nothing remains. (This will help remove any oils and excess moisture from the bowl.) Let dry.

**2.** In the top of a double boiler, whisk together egg whites and granulated sugar. Cook over simmering water, whisking frequently, until sugar fully dissolves and an instant-read thermometer registers 150°F (65°C). (Sugar is dissolved when you can rub the mixture between your fingers and feel no sugar.)

**3.** Transfer egg white mixture to the cleaned stand mixer bowl. Fit stand mixer with the whisk attachment, and beat on low speed, increasing mixer speed to medium as mixture becomes bubbly. Beat until stiff peaks form and meringue is glossy and white, 7 to 10 minutes. Add butter, 2 tablespoons (28 grams) at a time, beating until combined after each addition. Add confectioners' sugar, vanilla bean paste, and salt, beating until fully combined, about 1 minute.

**4.** Switch to the paddle attachment. Beat on low speed to remove any air bubbles, 2 to 3 minutes.

# browned butter

MAKES ABOUT ¾ CUP

1 cup (227 grams) unsalted butter, cubed

**1.** In a small saucepan, melt butter over medium-low heat, and cook, stirring occasionally, until browned and foamy. (Browned bits should appear on bottom of pan underneath foam, and the color should be a deep golden brown.) Remove from heat, and use as directed in recipe.

## salted caramel

MAKES ABOUT 1½ CUPS

- 1 cup (200 grams) granulated sugar
- 6 tablespoons (84 grams) unsalted butter
- ½ cup (120 grams) warm heavy whipping cream
- ½ to 1 teaspoon (1.5 to 3 grams) kosher salt, to taste

**1.** In a medium skillet, heat sugar over medium-low heat, stirring occasionally, until completely melted and all clumps are gone. Add butter, and reduce heat to low. Cook, gently whisking constantly, until butter is melted, 2 to 3 minutes. (The mixture may stiffen a bit, but this is normal; simply continue to whisk.) Add warm cream, whisking until combined. (If the sauce separates, this is normal; again, continue to whisk.) Increase heat to medium, and cook, whisking constantly, until sauce comes together and is smooth, 2 to 3 minutes. Remove from heat as soon as sauce comes back together. Whisk in salt. Pour into a heatproof container, and let cool completely.

# pastry cream

MAKES ABOUT 2½ CUPS

1¼ cups (300 grams) whole milk
1 cup (240 grams) heavy whipping cream
6 large egg yolks (114 grams)
½ cup (100 grams) granulated sugar
6 tablespoons (48 grams) cornstarch
2 tablespoons (28 grams) unsalted butter
2 teaspoons (12 grams) vanilla bean paste
Pinch kosher salt

1. In a medium saucepan, heat milk and cream over low heat until just warmed all the way through (about 105°F/41°C), 5 to 7 minutes.
2. In a medium bowl, whisk together egg yolks, sugar, and cornstarch until a thick paste forms. Slowly add warm milk mixture, about ½ cup (120 grams) at a time, whisking constantly to prevent egg yolks from cooking. Once all milk mixture is added, pour mixture back into the saucepan. Increase heat to medium, and bring to a boil, whisking constantly. Remove from heat, and whisk vigorously for 1 minute. Add butter, vanilla bean paste, and salt, whisking until butter is fully melted. Strain through a fine-mesh sieve into a rimmed baking sheet. Cover with plastic wrap, pressing wrap directly onto surface of pastry cream to prevent a film from forming. Refrigerate until set, 1 to 2 hours.

NOTE: *This pastry cream is developed with mixing in liquids in mind. Throughout the book, you'll find me adding things like juice or rum. If you just want a traditional pastry cream, whisk in ¼ cup (60 grams) whole milk after the mixture is set.*

# banana milk alternative

1¼ cups (300 grams) whole milk
1 cup (240 grams) heavy whipping cream
4 very ripe bananas (about 341 grams), lightly mashed

1. In a small saucepan, heat milk and cream over medium-low heat until simmering. Transfer to a heatproof medium bowl, and stir in bananas until bananas are fully submerged. Let cool to room temperature. Cover and refrigerate for at least 4 hours to infuse milk mixture with banana flavor.
2. Using a fine-mesh sieve, strain milk mixture into a medium saucepan, mashing bananas to make sure you get as much of the liquid as possible. Use in place of the milk and heavy cream in Pastry Cream recipe (above).

NOTE: *This milk alternative is a great way to add flavor to the basic Pastry Cream (recipe above). I love to use this for my Banana Rum Cream Brioche Doughnuts (recipe on page 34) and my Banana Pudding Pavlova (recipe on page 82).*

PASTRY CREAM

BANANA MILK ALTERNATIVE

# cake release

MAKES ABOUT 1½ CUPS

- ½ cup (63 grams) all-purpose flour
- ½ cup (112 grams) vegetable oil
- ½ cup (96 grams) all-vegetable shortening

**1.** In a large bowl, beat all ingredients with a handheld mixer on medium speed until combined. Store in an airtight container until ready to use.

**NOTE:** *This is my secret weapon to ensuring my cakes don't stick! Simply brush it on your favorite cake pans before baking. Once you try this, you'll never go back to store-bought baking spray again.*

# a morning pick-me-up

# banana rum cream brioche doughnuts

**MAKES 15 DOUGHNUTS**

*Fried to perfection, these are the ultimate brioche-style doughnut. Pillowy, light, and filled with an enticing banana rum cream, these are the best way to start your day.*

**TANGZHONG:**
- 1 cup (240 grams) whole milk
- 5 tablespoons (40 grams) all-purpose flour

**DOUGHNUTS:**
- ½ cup (120 grams) warm whole milk (105°F/41°C to 110°F/43°C)
- ½ cup (100 grams) granulated sugar, divided
- 2¼ teaspoons (7 grams) active dry yeast
- 1 large egg (50 grams), room temperature
- 1 large egg yolk (19 grams), room temperature
- 1 teaspoon (3 grams) kosher salt
- 4½ cups (563 grams) all-purpose flour, plus more for dusting
- ½ cup (113 grams) salted butter, room temperature

Vegetable oil, for frying
Granulated sugar, for coating

**FILLING:**
Pastry Cream with Banana Milk Alternative (recipe on page 30)
2 tablespoons (30 grams) dark rum

**PRO TIP:** *Pinch off a piece of the dough, and gently stretch it between two fingers. If you can see through it, the dough is ready. If the dough breaks, continue to beat for 2 minutes and then repeat the windowpane test.*

**1.** For the tangzhong: In a small saucepan, heat milk over medium heat until scalding, about 5 minutes. Whisk in flour, and cook, whisking constantly, until a thick paste forms, 2 to 3 minutes. (The texture should be akin to thick porridge.) Transfer to a small heatproof bowl. Let cool completely.

**2.** For the doughnuts: In the bowl of a stand mixer, stir together warm milk, 1 tablespoon (12 grams) sugar, and yeast by hand. Let stand until bloomed and foaming, 5 to 10 minutes. Add tangzhong, egg, egg yolk, salt, and remaining ¼ cup plus 3 tablespoons (86 grams) sugar, and whisk by hand until well combined. Using your hands (or a silicone spatula), gently fold in flour until a shaggy dough forms.

**3.** Fit stand mixer with the dough hook attachment, and knead dough on medium speed until dough begins to smooth, 5 to 7 minutes. Add butter, 2 tablespoons (28 grams) at a time, kneading after each addition until no streaks of butter remain, about 45 seconds each. Continue to knead until dough is smooth and elastic, about 10 minutes. Stop mixer, and perform the windowpane test. (See Pro Tip).

**4.** Place dough in a well-oiled bowl. Cover and let rise in a warm, draft-free place (75°F/24°C) until doubled in size, 1½ to 2 hours.

**5.** Punch down dough; turn out onto a well-floured surface. Divide into 15 equal pieces. Shape each piece into a smooth ball, then pressing slightly to form a disk. Place on a parchment lined baking sheet, and cover. Let rise in a warm, draft-free place (75°F/24°C) until puffed, 30 to 45 minutes.

**6.** In a large heavy-bottomed pot, pour oil to a depth of 2 inches, and heat over medium heat until a deep-fry thermometer registers 350°F (180°C). Line 2 large rimmed baking sheets with paper towels.

**7.** Fry doughnuts in batches until golden brown, 2 to 3 minutes per side. Using a spider strainer or slotted spoon, remove doughnuts from oil, and let drain on prepared pans. Let cool for 5 minutes. Toss in sugar to coat. Transfer to a wire rack, and let cool completely.

**8.** For the filling: Place prepared Pastry Cream with Banana Milk Alternative in a medium bowl, and whisk until smooth. Add rum, and whisk until combined. Transfer to a 12-inch pastry bag fitted with your favorite piping tip.

**9.** Make a pocket in each cooled doughnut by inserting a small knife in one side and moving it back and forth slightly. Pipe a generous amount of filling into each doughnut.

# blueberry pancake muffins

MAKES 12 MUFFINS

*If maple syrup-covered pancakes and blueberry muffins had a baby, these muffins would be it. A maple glaze infuses every bite with a woody sweetness while plump blueberries add a bright burst of freshness.*

MUFFINS:
- 2¾ cups (344 grams) all-purpose flour
- 2 cups (300 grams) fresh blueberries
- 1 tablespoon (15 grams) baking powder
- ½ teaspoon (2.5 grams) baking soda
- ½ teaspoon (1.5 grams) kosher salt
- 1 cup (200 grams) granulated sugar
- ½ cup (110 grams) firmly packed light brown sugar
- ½ cup (113 grams) salted butter, melted
- ½ cup (112 grams) vegetable oil
- 2 large eggs (100 grams), room temperature
- ½ cup (120 grams) whole buttermilk, room temperature
- ⅓ cup (80 grams) sour cream, room temperature
- 1 tablespoon (13 grams) maple extract
- 1 teaspoon (6 grams) vanilla bean paste

GLAZE:
- 1 cup (120 grams) confectioners' sugar
- ¼ cup (57 grams) salted butter, melted and cooled slightly
- 2 tablespoons (42 grams) maple syrup
- 1 to 2 tablespoons (15 to 30 grams) heavy whipping cream
- 1 teaspoon (6 grams) vanilla bean paste

**1.** For the muffins: In a medium bowl, stir together flour, blueberries, baking powder, baking soda, and salt.

**2.** In another medium bowl, whisk together granulated sugar, brown sugar, melted butter, oil, and eggs until sugars begin to dissolve, 2 to 3 minutes. Add buttermilk, sour cream, maple extract, and vanilla bean paste. Whisk until smooth. Using a silicone spatula, stir in flour mixture until just combined. Cover and refrigerate for at least 1 hour, ideally overnight.

**3.** Preheat oven to 425°F (220°C). Place muffin liners in every other cup of 2 (12-cup) muffin pans. In empty cups, add ¼ cup (60 grams) water.

**4.** Spoon batter into prepared muffin cups, filling to top of liners.

**5.** Bake for 5 minutes. Reduce oven temperature to 350°F (180°C), and bake until golden brown and a wooden pick inserted in center comes out clean, 15 to 18 minutes more. Let cool in pans for 10 minutes. Remove from pans, and place on wire rack.

**6.** For the glaze: In a small bowl, whisk together all ingredients, adding enough cream to reach desired consistency. Drizzle on top of muffins.

# wake-me-up cappuccino cake

**MAKES 1 (8-INCH) CAKE**

*Who needs a morning cup of coffee when you can have a slice of cake? Get your daily dose of caffeine with layers of espresso-infused cake covered in a lush mascarpone frosting.*

## CAKE:

- 1¾ cups (420 grams) heavy whipping cream
- 2 tablespoons (12 grams) espresso powder, divided
- 1 tablespoon (18 grams) vanilla bean paste
- 3 cups (375 grams) all-purpose flour
- 1 tablespoon (15 grams) baking powder
- ½ teaspoon (1.5 grams) kosher salt
- ½ teaspoon (1 gram) ground nutmeg
- ¼ teaspoon (1.25 grams) baking soda
- ¾ cup (170 grams) unsalted butter, room temperature
- 2 cups (400 grams) granulated sugar
- ½ cup (110 grams) firmly packed light brown sugar
- 4 large eggs (200 grams), room temperature
- ½ cup (120 grams) sour cream, room temperature

## FROSTING:

- 3 cups (360 grams) confectioners' sugar
- 3 cups (720 grams) cold heavy whipping cream
- 12 ounces (340 grams) cold mascarpone cheese
- 1½ tablespoons (27 grams) vanilla bean paste
- 2½ teaspoons (5 grams) espresso powder

Unsweetened cocoa powder, for dusting

**1.** For the cake: In a small saucepan, heat cream over medium-low heat until simmering, 5 to 10 minutes. Add 1 tablespoon (6 grams) espresso powder and vanilla bean paste. Whisk until no clumps of espresso powder remain, 20 to 30 seconds; continue to simmer for 5 minutes. Remove from heat. Let cool for 30 minutes.

**2.** Preheat oven to 350°F (180°C). Using a pastry brush, brush 4 (8-inch) round cake pans with Cake Release (recipe on page 31) or spray with baking spray with flour.

**3.** In a large bowl, whisk together flour, baking powder, salt, nutmeg, baking soda, and remaining 1 tablespoon (6 grams) espresso powder.

**4.** In the bowl of a stand mixer fitted with the paddle attachment, beat butter, granulated sugar, and brown sugar on medium speed until fluffy, about 5 minutes, scraping down sides of bowl. Add eggs, one at a time, ensuring each egg is fully incorporated prior to adding the next. Add sour cream, and continue to beat until well combined. With mixer on medium speed, gradually add cream mixture alternately with flour mixture, beginning with cream mixture and ending with flour mixture, beating until just combined after each addition. Divide batter among prepared pans.

**5.** Bake until a wooden pick inserted in center comes out clean, 28 to 30 minutes. Let cool in pans for 15 minutes. Remove from pans. Let cool completely on wire racks.

**6.** For the frosting: In the bowl of a stand mixer fitted with the whisk attachment, beat confectioners' sugar, cream, mascarpone, and vanilla bean paste on low speed until just combined. Increase mixer speed to medium-high, and beat until stiff peaks form. Add espresso powder, and continue to beat until just combined.

**7.** Place 1 cooled cake layer on a cake stand. Spread an even layer of frosting onto cake layer. Top with a second cake layer. Repeat until all layers are added. Spread a thin layer of frosting on top and sides of cake. Transfer remaining frosting to a 12-inch pastry bag fitted with your favorite piping tip. Pipe top and sides of cake. Dust with cocoa powder.

# *mocha swirl buns*
## WITH COFFEE CREAM CHEESE GLAZE
### MAKES 12 BUNS

*Combining the delicate texture of Japanese milk bread from the tangzhong with bold swirls of mocha, these buns are ideal for coffee lovers seeking a sophisticated version of traditional sweet rolls.*

**TANGZHONG:**
- ¾ cup (180 grams) whole milk
- ⅓ cup (42 grams) bread flour

**DOUGH:**
- ½ cup (120 grams) warm whole milk (105°F/41°C to 110°F/43°C)
- ½ cup (100 grams) plus 1 tablespoon (12 grams) granulated sugar, divided
- 2¼ teaspoons (7 grams) active dry yeast
- 1 large egg (50 grams), room temperature
- 1 large egg yolk (19 grams), room temperature
- 1 teaspoon (3 grams) kosher salt
- 4½ cups (572 grams) bread flour, plus more for dusting
- ½ cup (113 grams) unsalted butter, room temperature

**FILLING:**
- ¾ cup (165 grams) firmly packed light brown sugar
- ½ cup (113 grams) unsalted butter, room temperature
- 2 tablespoons (10 grams) unsweetened cocoa powder
- 2 tablespoons (30 grams) heavy whipping cream
- 1½ teaspoons (3 grams) espresso powder
- Pinch kosher salt

Unsalted butter, for coating pan

**ICING:**
- 1 (8-ounce) package (226 grams) cream cheese, room temperature
- 2 tablespoons (28 grams) unsalted butter, room temperature
- 2 teaspoons (12 grams) vanilla bean paste
- 3 cups (360 grams) confectioners' sugar

Unsweetened cocoa powder, to serve

1. For the tangzhong: In a small saucepan, heat milk over medium heat until scalding, about 5 minutes. Whisk in flour, and cook, whisking constantly, until a thick paste forms, 2 to 3 minutes. (The texture should be akin to thick porridge.) Transfer to small heatproof bowl. Let cool completely.

2. For the dough: In the bowl of a stand mixer, stir together warm milk, 1 tablespoon (12 grams) sugar, and yeast by hand. Let stand until bloomed and foaming, 5 to 10 minutes. Add tangzhong, egg, egg yolk, salt, and remaining ½ cup (100 grams) sugar, and whisk by hand until well combined. Using your hands (or a silicone spatula), gently fold in flour until a shaggy dough forms.

3. Fit stand mixer with the dough hook attachment, and knead dough on medium speed until dough begins to smooth, 5 to 7 minutes. Add butter, 2 tablespoons (28 grams) at a time, kneading after each addition until no streaks of butter remain, about 45 seconds each. Continue to knead until dough is smooth and elastic, about 10 minutes. Stop mixer, and perform the windowpane test. (See Pro Tip on page 35.)

4. Place dough in a well-oiled bowl. Cover and let rise in a warm, draft-free place (75°F/24°C) until doubled in size, 1½ to 2 hours.

5. For the filling: In a medium bowl, stir together all ingredients until well combined, 1 to 2 minutes.

6. Generously coat 2 (6-cup) jumbo muffin pans with butter.

7. Punch down dough. Turn out onto a well-floured surface, and roll into an 18-inch square. Spread filling onto dough in an even layer, coating entire surface. Using a serrated knife, slice dough into 12 strips. Roll each strip into a spiral, and place, spiral side down, in prepared muffin cups. Cover and let rise in a warm, draft-free place (75°F/24°C) until puffed, 30 to 45 minutes.

8. Preheat oven to 350°F (180°C).

9. Bake until golden brown, 20 to 25 minutes. Let cool in pans, 3 to 5 minutes. Remove from pans.

10. For the icing: In the bowl of a stand mixer fitted with the paddle attachment, beat cream cheese, butter, and vanilla bean paste on medium-low speed for 2 minutes. Add confectioners' sugar, and gradually increase mixer speed to medium, beating until smooth, 1 to 2 minutes. Spread icing onto warm buns. Lightly dust with cocoa powder to serve.

# chamomile sugar muffins

### MAKES 12 MUFFINS

*With a golden exterior shimmering with aromatic chamomile sugar crystals, these muffins are a delightful fusion of floral sweetness and citrusy brightness, evoking memories of tranquil mornings luxriating in the sun.*

MUFFINS:
- 1 cup (240 grams) whole milk
- 3 tea bags chamomile tea*
- ½ cup (113 grams) unsalted butter
- 1¼ cups (250 grams) granulated sugar
- 1 tablespoon (6 grams) orange zest
- 2 large eggs (100 grams), room temperature
- ⅓ cup (80 grams) sour cream, room temperature
- ¼ cup (56 grams) vegetable oil
- 2 teaspoons (8 grams) vanilla extract
- 2½ cups (313 grams) all-purpose flour
- 1 tablespoon (15 grams) baking powder
- 1 teaspoon (2 grams) ground ginger
- ½ teaspoon (2.5 grams) baking soda
- ½ teaspoon (1.5 grams) kosher salt

TOPPING:
- 3 tea bags chamomile tea
- ½ cup (100 grams) granulated sugar
- ¼ cup (57 grams) unsalted butter, melted

1. For the muffins: In a small saucepan, heat milk and tea bags over low heat until simmering; add butter, and simmer, stirring occasionally, until butter is melted. Remove from heat, and let steep for 20 minutes; squeeze excess milk from tea bags, and discard tea bags.
2. In a large bowl, pinch together sugar and orange zest until sugar is pale orange and fragrant. Add eggs, sour cream, and oil. Whisk until sugar begins to dissolve and mixture is smooth, about 2 minutes. Whisk in chamomile milk mixture and vanilla extract.
3. In a medium bowl, whisk together flour, baking powder, ginger, baking soda, and salt. Add the dry ingredients to the wet ingredients, and stir until combined. Cover with plastic wrap, and refrigerate for 2 hours.
4. Preheat oven to 425°F (220°C). Place muffin liners in every other cup of 2 (12-cup) muffin pans. In empty cups, add ¼ cup (60 grams) water.
5. Spoon batter into prepared muffin cups, filling to top of liners.
6. Bake for 5 minutes. Reduce oven temperature to 350°F (180°C), and bake until golden brown and a wooden pick inserted in center comes out clean, 12 to 13 minutes more. Let cool in pans for 5 to 10 minutes. Remove from pans, and let cool completely on a wire rack.
7. For the topping: Cut open tea bags, and add tea leaves to a medium bowl. Add sugar, and mix together. Brush tops of cooled muffins with melted butter, and coat with chamomile sugar.

*I use Harney & Sons Classic Chamomile Herbal Tea.

# café au lait beignets

**MAKES 20 BEIGNETS**

*A tasty twist on a New Orleans favorite, pillowy-soft dough is fried and generously filled with a luscious coffee-flavored pastry cream. Whether enjoyed as a breakfast treat or a tempting midday pick-me-up, these beignets are a celebration of flavors that will awaken your senses and leave you craving more.*

### BEIGNETS:

- 2 cups (254 grams) bread flour
- 2 cups (250 grams) all-purpose flour, plus more for dusting
- 2 teaspoons (4 grams) espresso powder
- 1 teaspoon (3 grams) kosher salt
- 1 teaspoon (2 grams) ground cinnamon
- ½ teaspoon (1 gram) ground nutmeg
- ¼ teaspoon (1.25 grams) baking powder
- ½ cup (120 grams) warm whole milk (105°F/41°C to 110°F/43°C)
- 4 tablespoons (48 grams) granulated sugar
- 1½ teaspoons (4.5 grams) active dry yeast
- ½ cup (120 grams) evaporated milk
- 1 large egg (50 grams), room temperature
- 1 large egg white (30 grams), room temperature
- ¼ cup (57 grams) unsalted butter, room temperature

### FILLING:

- 1 cup (240 grams) cold heavy whipping cream
- ⅓ cup (40 grams) confectioners' sugar
- 1 tablespoon (6 grams) espresso powder

Pastry Cream (recipe on page 30)

Vegetable oil, for frying
Confectioners' sugar, to serve

**1.** For the beignets: In a medium bowl, whisk together flours, espresso powder, salt, cinnamon, nutmeg, and baking powder until well combined.

**2.** In the bowl of a stand mixer, stir together warm milk, 1 tablespoon (12 grams) sugar, and yeast by hand. Let stand until bloomed and foaming, 5 to 10 minutes. Add evaporated milk, egg, egg white, and remaining 3 tablespoons (36 grams) sugar, and whisk by hand until well combined. Using your hands (or a silicone spatula), gently fold in flour-mixture until a shaggy dough forms.

**3.** Fit stand mixer with the dough hook attachment, and knead dough on medium speed until dough begins to smooth, 5 to 7 minutes. Add butter, 2 tablespoons (28 grams) at a time, kneading after each addition until no streaks of butter remain, about 45 seconds each. Continue to knead until dough is smooth and elastic, about 10 minutes. Stop mixer, and perform the windowpane test. (See Pro Tip on page 35.)

**4.** Place dough in a well-oiled bowl. Cover and let rise in a warm, draft-free place (75°F/24°C) until doubled in size, 1½ to 2 hours.

**5.** Punch down dough. Refrigerate overnight. (The second proof needs a minimum of 8 hours, but 24 hours is ideal.)

**6.** For the filling: In the bowl of a stand mixer fitted with the whisk attachment, beat cold cream, confectioners' sugar, and espresso powder on medium-high speed until medium peaks form. Add half of Pastry Cream, and continue to beat until fully combined. Repeat with remaining Pastry Cream. Cover and refrigerate until ready to use.

**7.** Turn out dough onto lightly floured surface, and roll into a 15x12-inch rectangle (about ¼ inch thick). Using a sharp kitchen knife, cut into 3-inch squares. Cover, and let rise in a warm, draft-free place (75°F/24°C) until puffed, 30 to 45 minutes.

**8.** In a large heavy-bottomed pot, pour oil to a depth of 2 inches, and heat over medium heat until a deep-fry thermometer registers 350°F (180°C). Line 2 large rimmed baking sheets with paper towels.

**9.** Fy beignets in batches until puffed and golden brown, 1 to 2 minutes per side. Using a spider strainer or slotted spoon, remove doughnuts from oil, and let drain on prepared pans.Let cool completely.

**10.** Transfer filling to a pastry bag fitted with your favorite piping tip.

**11.** Make a pocket in each cooled doughnut by inserting a small knife in one side and moving it back and forth slightly. Pipe a generous amount of filling into each doughnut. Generously dust with confectioners' sugar to serve.

# chocolate tart
## WITH ESPRESSO WHIPPED CREAM

MAKES 1 (14X4½-INCH) TART

*A silky ganache filling is complemented by the light, airy espresso-infused whipped cream, all nestled within a buttery graham cracker crust that balances the texture and rounds out the flavor in this lavish dessert.*

CRUST:
- 10 graham cracker sheets (150 grams)
- 2 tablespoons (24 grams) granulated sugar
- ½ teaspoon (1 gram) ground cinnamon
- ½ teaspoon (1 gram) espresso powder
- ⅓ cup (76 grams) unsalted butter, melted
- ¼ teaspoon kosher salt

FILLING:
- 8 ounces (226 grams) quality dark chocolate, chopped
- ¾ cup (180 grams) heavy whipping cream

WHIPPED CREAM:
- 1 cup (240 grams) cold heavy whipping cream
- ½ cup (60 grams) confectioners' sugar
- 1 teaspoon (6 grams) vanilla bean paste
- ¾ teaspoon (1.5 grams) espresso powder

Unsweetened cocoa powder, to serve

**1.** For the crust: In the bowl of a food processor, process graham crackers, granulated sugar, cinnamon, and espresso powder until fine, uniform crumbs form. With food processor running, add melted butter. Stop and scrape down sides of bowl. Continue to process until texture resembles wet sand, about 1 minute. Using the bottom of a cup, press mixture into bottom and up sides of a 14x4½-inch fluted tart pan with removable bottom. Refrigerate until set, about 1 hour.

**2.** For the filling: In a medium heatproof glass bowl, place chocolate.

**3.** In a small saucepan, heat cream over medium-low heat until simmering, about 5 minutes. Pour over chocolate. Let stand for 2 minutes. Stir until chocolate is fully melted and mixture is combined. Pour into prepared crust. Using an offset spatula, spread chocolate mixture into an even layer until smooth. Refrigerate until set, at least 30 minutes.

**4.** For the whipped cream: In a large bowl, whisk together all ingredients until stiff peaks form. Transfer to a pastry bag fitted with your favorite piping tip. Pipe on top of filling. Dust with cocoa powder.

> *life is short.*
> *eat dessert*
> *first.*
>
> — JACQUES TORRES

# the ultimate cinnamon rolls

MAKES 12 ROLLS

*Light and fluffy, with a gooey cinnamon-swirled center, these sumptuous rolls are topped with a cream cheese icing, making them an irresistible treat any time of day.*

DOUGH:
- 4 cups (508 grams) bread flour, plus more for dusting
- 2 cups (250 grams) cake flour
- 1½ cups (360 grams) whole milk, divided
- ½ cup (100 grams) plus 1 tablespoon (12 grams) granulated sugar, divided
- 2 teaspoons (4 grams) ground cinnamon
- 1¾ teaspoons (5.25 grams) kosher salt
- ¼ teaspoon ground nutmeg
- 1 tablespoon (9 grams) active dry yeast
- 3 large eggs (150 grams), room temperature
- 1 teaspoon (6 grams) vanilla bean paste
- 1 cup (227 grams) salted butter, room temperature

FILLING:
- 1 cup (220 grams) firmly packed dark brown sugar
- ½ cup (113 grams) unsalted butter, room temperature
- 2½ tablespoons (15 grams) ground cinnamon
- Pinch kosher salt
- ⅓ cup (80 grams) heavy whipping cream

ICING:
- 6 ounces (170 grams) cream cheese, room temperature
- ½ cup (113 grams) unsalted butter, room temperature
- 2 cups (240 grams) confectioners' sugar
- 3 to 6 tablespoons (45 to 90 grams) heavy whipping cream
- 2 teaspoons (12 grams) vanilla bean paste
- Pinch kosher salt

**1.** For the dough: In a large bowl, whisk together flours.
**2.** In the bowl of a stand mixer, stir together 3 cups (375 grams) flour mixture and 1 cup (240 grams) milk with a silicone spatula until well combined. Cover and let stand for 30 minutes.
**3.** Add ½ cup (100 grams) granulated sugar, cinnamon, salt, and nutmeg to flour-milk mixture; whisk until combined.
**4.** In a heatproof bowl, microwave remaining ½ cup (120 grams) milk on high until warm (105°F/41°C to 110°F/43°C). Add yeast and remaining 1 tablespoon (12 grams) granulated sugar; whisk until combined. Let stand until bloomed and foaming, 5 to 10 minutes. Add eggs and vanilla bean paste, and whisk until well combined.
**5.** Add yeast mixture and remaining flour mixture to flour-milk mixture. Using your hands, gently knead ingredients together, focusing on incorporating the rested flour-milk mixture into flour and yeast mixtures.
**6.** Fit stand mixer with the paddle attachment. Beat on medium-low speed until dough begins to form, about 5 minutes.
**7.** Switch to the dough hook attachment, and knead until dough becomes smooth, 3 to 5 minutes. Add butter, 2 tablespoons (28 grams) at a time, kneading until combined after each addition, about 45 seconds. Continue to knead until smooth, about 5 minutes. Stop mixer, and

perform the windowpane test. (See Pro Tip on page 35.)

**8.** Place dough in a well-oiled bowl. Cover, and let rise in a warm, draft-free place (75°F/24°C) until doubled in size, about 1½ hours.

**9.** For the filling: In a small bowl, stir together brown sugar, butter, cinnamon, and salt. Spoon 2 tablespoons filling into a 13x9-inch baking pan. Using your fingers, rub filling along bottom and sides of pan until a thin film coats pan.

**10.** Lightly dust work surface with bread flour. Turn out dough onto surface, and stretch into an 18x12-inch rectangle. (Try to avoid using a rolling pin to keep as much air in the dough as possible.) Using an offset spatula, spread remaining filling onto dough. Using a sharp kitchen knife or pizza wheel, cut dough into 12 (1-inch) strips. Roll each strip into a tight spiral, and place, spiral side down, in prepared pan. Cover, and let rise in a warm, draft-free place (75°F/24°C) until puffy, 25 to 40 minutes.

**11.** Preheat oven to 350°F (180°C).

**12.** Pour cream on top of and around rolls.

**13.** Bake until rolls are golden brown, 40 to 45 minutes.

**14.** For the icing: In the bowl of a stand mixer fitted with the paddle attachment, beat cream cheese and butter on medium speed until creamy. With mixer on low speed, gradually add confectioners' sugar and cream until desired consistency is reached. Add vanilla bean paste and salt; continue to beat until well combined. Spread icing onto hot cinnamon rolls. (If you don't like melted icing, let cinnamon rolls cool for 30 to 45 minutes before adding the icing.)

# *classic banana bread*

MAKES 1 (9X5-INCH) LOAF

*A golden crust gives way to a soft, cake-like interior filled with the natural sweetness of bananas. Enjoy warm with a smear of butter or a drizzle of honey.*

Streusel:
- ¼ cup (55 grams) firmly packed light brown sugar
- 2 tablespoons (28 grams) salted butter, melted
- ½ teaspoon (1 gram) ground cinnamon
- 7 tablespoons (56 grams) all-purpose flour
- Pinch kosher salt

Bread:
- 1½ cups (375 grams) very ripe mashed bananas (about 4 medium bananas)
- ¾ cup (165 grams) firmly packed light brown sugar
- ⅔ cup (160 grams) sour cream, room temperature
- ¼ cup (50 grams) granulated sugar
- ¼ cup (57 grams) salted butter, melted
- ¼ cup (56 grams) vegetable oil
- 2 large eggs (100 grams), room temperature
- 1 teaspoon (4 grams) vanilla extract
- 2 cups (250 grams) all-purpose flour
- 1 teaspoon (5 grams) baking soda
- ½ teaspoon (1.5 grams) kosher salt
- ½ teaspoon (1 gram) ground cinnamon
- ⅛ teaspoon ground nutmeg
- 1 cup (113 grams) chopped walnuts

1. Preheat oven to 325°F (170°C). Line a 9x5-inch loaf pan with parchment paper, letting excess extend over sides of pan.
2. For the streusel: In a medium bowl, stir together brown sugar, melted butter, and cinnamon. Stir in flour and salt until crumbles form. Cover and refrigerate until ready to use.
3. For the bread: In a large bowl, whisk together bananas, brown sugar, sour cream, granulated sugar, melted butter, oil, eggs, and vanilla extract until smooth. Add flour, baking soda, salt, cinnamon, and nutmeg, stirring until smooth. Fold in walnuts. Pour batter into prepared pan. Sprinkle streusel on top.
4. Bake until a wooden pick inserted in center comes out clean, 1 hour and 20 minutes to 1½ hours. Let cool in pan for 20 minutes. Using excess parchment as handles, remove from pan, and let cool on a wire rack for 20 to 30 minutes.

# chai swiss roll

## WITH BROWNED BUTTER-CREAM CHEESE FILLING

#### MAKES 1 SWISS ROLL

*This is easily one of my favorite recipes! A classic Swiss roll is made even better with a chai spice-infused cake wrapped around browned butter-cream cheese frosting.*

CAKE:
- 1¾ cups (219 grams) cake flour
- 1 tablespoon (6 grams) ground cinnamon
- 1 teaspoon (5 grams) baking powder
- ½ teaspoon (1 gram) ground cardamom
- ½ teaspoon (1 gram) ground ginger
- ¼ teaspoon kosher salt
- ¼ teaspoon ground cloves
- ¼ teaspoon ground nutmeg
- Pinch ground black pepper
- 5 large eggs (250 grams), separated and room temperature
- ¼ teaspoon cream of tartar
- ½ cup plus 4 tablespoons (148 grams) granulated sugar, divided
- ½ cup (112 grams) vegetable oil
- ½ cup (120 grams) whole milk, room temperature

Confectioners' sugar, for dusting

FILLING:
- ¾ cup (156 grams) Browned Butter (recipe on page 28), room temperature
- 1 (8-ounce) package (226 grams) cream cheese, room temperature
- 3 cups plus 4 tablespoons (388 grams) confectioners' sugar, divided
- 1 tablespoon (10 grams) meringue powder
- 2 teaspoons (8 grams) vanilla extract
- Pinch kosher salt

1. Preheat oven to 325°F (170°C). Line an 18x13-inch rimmed baking sheet with parchment paper.

2. For the cake: In a small bowl, whisk together flour, cinnamon, baking powder, cardamom, ginger, salt, cloves, nutmeg, and pepper.

3. In the bowl of a stand mixer fitted with the whisk attachment, beat egg whites and cream of tartar on medium-low speed until bubbly, 1 to 2 minutes. With mixer running, slowly add 3 tablespoons (36 grams) granulated sugar. Increase mixer speed to medium, and beat until stiff peaks form, 5 to 7 minutes.

4. In a large bowl, beat egg yolks and remaining ½ cup plus 1 tablespoon (112 grams) granulated sugar with a handheld mixer on medium speed until bubbly and lighter in color, about 2 minutes. Add oil, and continue to beat until well combined, about 1 minute. Add milk, and continue to beat until well combined, about 1 minute. Gradually add flour mixture alternately with meringue, beginning and ending with flour mixture, folding with a silicone spatula until just combined after each addition. Pour batter into prepared pan. Using an offset spatula, spread smooth. Tap pan on a kitchen towel-lined counter to release excess air bubbles.

5. Bake until a wooden pick inserted in center comes out clean, 20 to 22 minutes. Using a fine-mesh sieve, dust confectioners' sugar on top of cake. Top with a clean kitchen towel and a cutting board. Invert cake onto cutting board. Starting with one short side, roll up cake with towel into a spiral. Let cool completely, 45 minutes to 1 hour.

6. For the filling: In the bowl of a stand mixer fitted with the paddle attachment, beat Browned Butter on medium-low speed until fluffy, about 2 minutes. Add cream cheese, and continue to beat until smooth, about 1 minute. Add 3 cups plus 2 tablespoons (374 grams) confectioners' sugar, meringue powder, vanilla, and salt. Gradually increase mixer speed to medium-low, and beat until smooth, 1 to 2 minutes.

7. Unroll cooled cake. Using an offset spatula, spread filling into an even layer on top of cake. Reroll cake without towel, tucking tightly to ensure a swirl without pressing too hard. Refrigerate until set, at least 1 hour. Using a fine-mesh sieve, dust with confectioners' sugar.

# glazed coconut financiers

**MAKES 16 FINANCIERS**

*These petite treats overflow with the nuttiness of almond and the tropical sweetness of coconut and are then crowned with a velvety coconut glaze. The buttery, moist crumb and crisp edges add unexpected luxury to a classic confection.*

**FINANCIERS:**
- 1 cup (96 grams) almond flour
- ⅔ cup (133 grams) granulated sugar
- ⅓ cup (42 grams) all-purpose flour
- 3 tablespoons (15 grams) sweetened flaked coconut, plus more for topping
- ¾ teaspoon (2.25 grams) kosher salt
- ¼ teaspoon (1.25 grams) baking powder
- 4 large egg whites (120 grams)
- 6 tablespoons (84 grams) Browned Butter (recipe on page 28), room temperature
- 1 tablespoon (21 grams) honey
- 1½ teaspoons (6 grams) coconut emulsion
- ½ teaspoon (3 grams) vanilla bean paste

**GLAZE:**
- 1¼ cups (150 grams) confectioners' sugar
- 4 to 5 tablespoons (60 to 75 grams) heavy whipping cream
- 1 teaspoon (4 grams) coconut emulsion

**1.** Preheat oven to 375°F (190°C). Using a pastry brush, brush 2 (8-well) financier pans with Cake Release (recipe on page 31) or spray with baking spray with flour. (If using a nonstick financier pan, no need to spray.)

**2.** For the financiers: In a large bowl, whisk together almond flour, granulated sugar, all-purpose flour, flaked coconut, salt, and baking powder. Add egg whites, Browned Butter, honey, coconut emulsion, and vanilla bean paste. Whisk until just combined. Spoon mixture into prepared wells, filling about three-fourths full.

**3.** Bake until center springs back when pressed, about 12 minutes. Let cool in pan for 5 minutes. Remove from pan, and let cool completely on a wire rack.

**4.** For the glaze: In a medium bowl, whisk together confectioners' sugar, cream, and coconut emulsion until desired consistency. Dip top of each cooled financier into glaze. Let excess drip off. Top with flaked coconut. Place on wire rack to set.

# earl grey cake
## WITH CITRUS-ALMOND BUTTERCREAM

MAKES 1 (8-INCH) CAKE

*This refined and aromatic treat promises to enchant tea lovers. Each layer overflows with the distinct, floral notes of Earl Grey tea, offering a subtle bergamot fragrance that pairs well with the brightness of the citrus-almond buttercream.*

### SIMPLE SYRUP:
- ¾ cup (150 grams) granulated sugar
- ¾ cup (180 grams) water
- 2 tea bags Earl Grey tea

### CAKE:
- 2 cups (480 grams) heavy whipping cream
- 12 tea bags Earl Grey tea
- ¾ cup (180 grams) whole milk, room temperature
- ¼ cup (60 grams) sour cream, room temperature
- 3 cups (375 grams) all-purpose flour
- 1 tablespoon (15 grams) baking powder
- ½ teaspoon (2.5 grams) baking soda
- ½ teaspoon (1.5 grams) kosher salt
- ¼ teaspoon ground nutmeg
- ¾ cup (170 grams) salted butter, room temperature
- 2¼ cups (450 grams) granulated sugar
- 4 large eggs (200 grams), room temperature
- 1 teaspoon (4 grams) vanilla extract
- 1 teaspoon (2 grams) orange zest

### BUTTERCREAM:
- 1 cup (227 grams) unsalted butter, room temperature
- 5 cups (600 grams) confectioners' sugar
- ¼ cup (60 grams) heavy whipping cream
- 1 tablespoon (6 grams) orange zest
- 1 teaspoon (4 grams) almond extract
- Pinch kosher salt

Garnish: loose-leaf Earl Grey tea, sliced almonds, dried culinary lavender, and orange slices

**1.** For the simple syrup: In a small saucepan, bring granulated sugar and ¾ cup (180 grams) water to a boil over high heat. Add tea bags, and continue to boil for 2 minutes. Reduce heat to low, and simmer for 5 minutes. Remove from heat. Let cool completely. Remove tea bags, pressing to remove extra liquid. Discard tea bags.

**2.** For the cake: In a small saucepan, heat cream over medium heat, stirring occasionally, until simmering. Add tea bags, and continue to simmer for 5 minutes. Remove from heat. Let steep for 1 hour. Remove tea bags, pressing to remove extra liquid. Discard tea bags.

**3.** Whisk in milk and sour cream into cream mixture until fully combined.

**4.** Preheat oven to 350°F (180°C). Using a pastry brush, brush 4 (8-inch) round cake pans with Cake Release (recipe on page 31) or spray with baking spray with flour.

**5.** In a medium bowl, whisk together flour, baking powder, baking soda, salt, and nutmeg.

**6.** In the bowl of a stand mixer fitted with the paddle attachment, beat butter and granulated sugar on medium speed until fully combined, about 2 minutes; scrape down sides of bowl. Continue to beat until lightened in color, about 2 minutes. Add eggs, one at a time, ensuring each egg is fully incorporated prior to adding the next. Scrape down sides and bottom of bowl. Add vanilla extract and orange zest. Continue to beat for 30 seconds more.

**7.** With mixer on low speed, gradually add cream mixture alternately with flour mixture, beginning with cream mixture and ending with flour mixture, beating until just combined after each addition. Scrape down sides and bottom of bowl. Stir mixture by hand to ensure it's evenly combined. Divide batter among prepared pans.

**8.** Bake until a wooden pick inserted in center comes out clean, 20 to 25 minutes. Let cool in pans for 10 minutes. Gently remove from pans, and place on wire racks. Brush with simple syrup, and let cool completely on wire racks.

**9.** For the buttercream: In the bowl of a stand mixer fitted with the paddle attachment, beat butter on medium speed until creamy, about 3 minutes. Gradually add confectioners' sugar, beating until a thick paste forms, 1 to 2 minutes. Add cream, orange zest, almond extract, and salt, and continue to beat until smooth and creamy, 3 to 5 minutes.

**10.** Place a small dollop of buttercream on center of a cake stand. Place 1 cooled cake layer on top of dollop. Spread an even layer of buttercream on top of cake layer. Top with second cake layer. Repeat until all cake layers are added. Spread remaining buttercream on top and sides of cake. Garnish with tea, almonds, lavender, and orange slices, if desired.

# buttery maple biscuits

## MAKES 9 BISCUITS

*Submerged in butter and then baked until golden brown, these biscuits practically melt in your mouth. The maple essence enhances each bite with a sweet yet woodsy aroma. Capturing the spirit of comfort baking, the subtle sweetness and satisfying crunch make these your new breakfast staple.*

- ½ cup (113 grams) unsalted butter
- 3 cups (375 grams) all-purpose flour
- 2 tablespoons (24 grams) granulated sugar
- 4 teaspoons (20 grams) baking powder
- 2 teaspoons (4 grams) ground cinnamon
- 1 teaspoon (3 grams) kosher salt
- ½ teaspoon (1 gram) ground nutmeg
- 1 cup (240 grams) sour cream
- 1 cup (240 grams) whole milk
- 3 tablespoons (63 grams) maple syrup
- 2 teaspoons (8 grams) maple extract

1. Preheat oven to 425°F (220°C). Place butter in a 9-inch square baking pan, and place pan in preheating oven. (Keep an eye on the butter to ensure it doesn't burn. Remove when the butter is fully melted.)

2. In a large bowl, whisk together flour, sugar, baking powder, cinnamon, salt, and nutmeg.

3. In a medium bowl, whisk together sour cream, milk, maple syrup, and maple extract. Add sour cream mixture to flour mixture, and stir with a silicone spatula or mix with your hands until just combined.

4. Remove pan from oven, and spread batter in an even layer in pan. Spoon some of the melted butter on top of batter to coat. Using a butter knife, cut 9 (3-inch) squares into batter.

5. Bake until tops are golden brown, 20 to 25 minutes. Let cool in pan for 10 minutes.

# fruity and fabulous

# apple bliss crisp

MAKES 8 SERVINGS

*I love all things apple throughout the year, and when fall arrives, my family loves to go apple picking. One year, I got the idea to turn my homemade apple cider into a concentrate to really up the apple flavor in my favorite apple crisp. It resulted in crisps that are perfectly spiced and very cinnamon-forward, with a golden-brown topping that provides a beautiful crunchy contrast to the tender apples.*

TOPPING:
- 1 cup (125 grams) all-purpose flour
- ¾ cup (165 grams) firmly packed light brown sugar
- 2 teaspoons (4 grams) ground cinnamon
- ¼ teaspoon ground nutmeg
- Pinch kosher salt
- ½ cup (113 grams) cold unsalted butter, cubed
- 1 cup (100 grams) old-fashioned oats

FILLING:
- 2 cups (480 grams) apple cider
- 1½ pounds (680 grams) Honeycrisp apples, peeled, cored, and cut into ½-inch slices
- 1 pound (453 grams) Granny Smith apples, peeled, cored, and cut into ½-inch slices
- ½ cup (110 grams) firmly packed light brown sugar
- 2 tablespoons (16 grams) cornstarch
- 1 tablespoon (6 grams) ground cinnamon
- 1 tablespoon (15 grams) fresh lemon juice
- 2 teaspoons (8 grams) vanilla extract
- ½ teaspoon (1 gram) ground nutmeg
- ½ teaspoon (1 gram) ground cloves
- ¼ teaspoon ground cardamom
- Pinch kosher salt

Vanilla ice cream or whipped cream, to serve

**1.** For the topping: In a medium bowl, stir together flour, brown sugar, cinnamon, nutmeg, and salt. Using your fingertips, cut in cold butter until pea-size pieces remain. Using your hands, mix in oats. Cover and refrigerate until ready to use.

**2.** For the filling: In a medium saucepan, cook apple cider over high heat, stirring frequently, until reduced to ¼ cup, 20 to 25 minutes.

**3.** Preheat oven to 350°F (180°C). Lightly spray a 2½-inch tall 10½-inch pie dish with cooking spray.

**4.** In a large bowl, stir together reduced cider, apples, brown sugar, cornstarch, cinnamon, lemon juice, vanilla extract, nutmeg, cloves, cardamom, and salt until apples are well coated. Spoon apple mixture into prepared pan. Crumble topping onto apple mixture.

**5.** Bake until apples are tender, topping is golden brown, and liquid is bubbling around the edge, 45 to 50 minutes. Serve warm with ice cream or whipped cream.

# salted caramel banana cake
## WITH CREAM CHEESE FROSTING

**MAKES 1 (8-INCH) CAKE**

*This moist banana cake is topped with a tangy cream cheese frosting and drizzled with ribbons of salted caramel. With each slice, you'll be left craving more.*

CAKE:
- 3¼ cups (406 grams) all-purpose flour
- 1½ teaspoons (7.5 grams) baking powder
- ½ teaspoon (2.5 grams) baking soda
- ½ teaspoon (1.5 grams) kosher salt
- ½ teaspoon (1 gram) ground cinnamon
- 1 cup (227 grams) unsalted butter, room temperature
- 2 cups (400 grams) granulated sugar
- 3 large eggs (150 grams), room temperature
- 1 teaspoon (4 grams) vanilla extract
- 1¾ cups (438 grams) very ripe mashed bananas (about 4 medium bananas)
- ½ cup (120 grams) sour cream, room temperature

FROSTING:
- ¾ cup (170 grams) unsalted butter, room temperature
- 12 ounces (340 grams) cream cheese, room temperature
- 5 cups (600 grams) confectioners' sugar
- 1 tablespoon (10 grams) meringue powder
- ⅛ teaspoon kosher salt
- 1 teaspoon (4 grams) vanilla extract

Salted Caramel (recipe on page 29)

**1.** Preheat oven to 350°F (180°C). Using a pastry brush, brush 3 (8-inch) round cake pans with Cake Release (recipe on page 31) or spray with baking spray with flour.

**2.** For the cake: In a medium bowl, whisk together flour, baking powder, baking soda, salt, and cinnamon.

**3.** In the bowl of a stand mixer fitted with the paddle attachment, beat butter on medium speed until smooth, about 2 minutes. Add granulated sugar, and continue to beat until fluffy, about 4 minutes, scraping down sides of bowl. Add eggs, one at a time, ensuring each egg is fully incorporated prior to adding the next. Scrape down sides of bowl, and beat in vanilla extract. Add banana, and continue to beat until well combined. (Batter may split, but it will come back together after the dry ingredients are added.) With mixer on low speed, add half of flour mixture, beating just until combined. Beat in sour cream. Add remaining flour mixture, beating just until combined. Divide batter among prepared pans.

**4.** Bake until golden brown and a wooden pick inserted in center comes out clean, 25 to 30 minutes. Let cool in pans for 5 minutes. Remove from pans, and let cool completely on wire racks.

**5.** For the frosting: In the bowl of a stand mixer fitted with the paddle attachment, beat butter at meadium speed until smooth and creamy, about 3 minutes. Add cream cheese, and continue to beat until well combined, about 2 minutes. With mixer on low speed, slowly add confectioners' sugar, meringue powder, and salt, beating until combined, scraping down sides of bowl. Add vanilla extract; increase mixer speed to medium, and beat until light and fluffy, about 2 minutes.

**6.** Place 1 cooled cake layer on a cake stand. Spread one-third of frosting on top, and drizzle with one-third of Salted Caramel. Repeat with remaining 2 cake layers, remaining frosting, and remaining Salted Caramel. Refrigerate for at least 30 minutes to set frosting.

# pomegranate crème brûlées

**MAKES 6 CRÈME BRÛLÉES**

*As you crack through the caramelized sugar topping, you're greeted with a burst of sweet and tart pomegranate custard that's both velvety and heavenly.*

CRÈME BRÛLÉES:
- 1 cup (240 grams) pomegranate juice
- 2 cups (480 grams) heavy whipping cream
- 6 large egg yolks (114 grams)
- ⅓ cup (67 grams) plus 6 teaspoons (24 grams) granulated sugar, divided

Boiling water

WHIPPED CREAM:
- 1 cup (240 grams) cold heavy whipping cream
- ¼ cup (30 grams) confectioners' sugar

Garnish: pomegranate arils

**1.** Preheat oven to 300°F (150°C).

**2.** For the crème brûlées: In a small saucepan, bring pomegranate juice to a boil over medium-high heat; boil until reduced to ¼ cup, 10 to 15 minutes. Reduce heat to low. Add cream, whisking slowly and constantly. Cook, whisking slowly and constantly, until cream is warmed through, 1 to 2 minutes. Remove from heat.

**3.** In a medium bowl, whisk together egg yolks and ⅓ cup (67 grams) granulated sugar until sugar dissolves and mixture is a pale yellow, 2 to 3 minutes. Slowly add pomegranate mixture, ½ cup at a time, whisking constantly to ensure the eggs do not cook.

**4.** Place 6 (6-ounce) ramekins in a baking pan. Spoon ½ cup (109 grams) custard into each ramekin. Place pan in oven. Pour boiling water into baking pan until water covers the bottom one-fourth of ramekins.

**5.** Bake until edges are set but centers are still jiggly and an instant-read thermometer inserted in center registers 175°F (79°C), 40 to 45 minutes*. Carefully, transfer ramekins to a wire rack, and let cool for 1 hour. Refrigerate for at least 4 hours, ideally overnight, to set.

**6.** Just before serving, sprinkle remaining 6 teaspoons (24 grams) granulated sugar on top of custards. Using a handheld kitchen torch, carefully brown the sugar.

**7.** For the whipped cream: In a large bowl, beat cold cream and confectioners' sugar with a handheld mixer on medium speed until medium peaks form. Dollop whipped cream on top of each crème brûlée. Garnish with pomegranate arils, if desired.

*\*If there is still liquid in the center, continue to bake for 5 to 10 minutes more.*

# more-crust-than-peaches peach cobbler

**MAKES 8 TO 10 SERVINGS**

I love peach cobbler, but I always find that I want more crust. For this recipe, a flaky piecrust is at the bottom layer, cinnamon-spiced peaches are in the middle, and then there's a crumble topping loaded with even more piecrust for the perfect bite! If you don't want all the extra goodness on top, skip step 5 and freeze the other half of the crust to use another day.

**CRUST:**
- 3 cups (375 grams) all-purpose flour, plus more for dusting
- 2 tablespoons (24 grams) granulated sugar
- 1½ teaspoons (4.5 grams) kosher salt
- 1 teaspoon (2 grams) ground cinnamon
- ½ teaspoon (1 gram) ground nutmeg
- 1 cup (227 grams) cold unsalted butter, cubed
- 8 to 10 tablespoons (120 to 150 grams) cold water

**TOPPING:**
- ¾ cup (94 grams) all-purpose flour
- ¼ cup (50 grams) granulated sugar
- 1 teaspoon (2 grams) ground cinnamon
- ¾ teaspoon (4 grams) baking powder
- ½ teaspoon (1.5 grams) kosher salt
- 10 tablespoons (140 grams) cold unsalted butter
- ⅓ cup (33 grams) old-fashioned oats

**FILLING:**
- 2 tablespoons (16 grams) cornstarch
- 2 tablespoons (30 grams) water
- 3 pounds (1,361 grams) fresh peaches, sliced
- 1 cup (200 grams) granulated sugar
- ⅔ cup (147 grams) firmly packed light brown sugar
- 2 tablespoons (30 grams) fresh lemon juice
- 1½ tablespoons (9 grams) ground cinnamon
- 1 teaspoon (2 grams) ground nutmeg
- ½ teaspoon (1.5 grams) kosher salt
- ½ teaspoon (1 gram) ground ginger
- ¼ cup (57 grams) unsalted butter

Vanilla ice cream or whipped cream, to serve

**1.** For the crust: In a large bowl, whisk together flour, granulated sugar, salt, cinnamon, and nutmeg. Using your fingertips, cut in cold butter until pea-size crumbs remain. Using your hands, mix in 8 tablespoons (120 grams) cold water until dough turns shaggy. (If dough is too dry, add up to 2 tablespoons [30 grams] cold water, 1 teaspoon [5 grams] at a time, as needed.)

**2.** Turn out dough onto a lightly floured surface. Knead dough until no shaggy bits remain. Cut dough in half (about 390 grams each), and pat each into a 4-inch square. Wrap both in plastic wrap, and refrigerate for at least 30 minutes.

**3.** Spray a 13x9-inch baking dish with baking spray with flour. Line a baking sheet with parchment paper.

**4.** Roll 1 dough square into a 14x10-inch rectangle, and place in bottom and up sides of prepared dish. Using a fork, poke holes every inch in bottom and sides of crust.

**5.** Roll remaining dough into a 14x10-inch rectangle, and cut into small, even strips. Place strips on a prepared baking sheet. Freeze both crusts for at least 20 minutes.

**6.** Preheat oven to 400°F (200°C).

**7.** Bake both crusts until golden brown, 20 to 25 minutes. Let cool. Reduce oven temperature to 375°F (190°C).

**8.** For the topping: In a large bowl, whisk together flour, granulated sugar, cinnamon, baking powder, and salt. Using your fingertips, cut in cold butter until pea-size crumbs remain. Using your hands, mix in oats until fully combined. Cover and refrigerate until ready to use.

**9.** For the filling: In a small bowl, stir together cornstarch and 2 tablespoons (30 grams) water until well combined.

**10.** In a medium saucepan, cook peaches, granulated sugar, brown sugar, lemon juice, cinnamon, nutmeg, salt, and ginger over medium heat, stirring occasionally, until juices bubble and peaches begin to soften, 10 minutes. Stir in cornstarch slurry, and continue to cook, stirring constantly, until mixture begins to thicken, 2 to 4 minutes. Remove from heat. Stir in butter until melted and fully combined. Pour into prepared crust. Crush crust strips on baking sheet into small pieces, and sprinkle on top of filling. Sprinkle topping onto filling.

**11.** Bake until topping is golden brown and filling is bubbly, 15 to 20 minutes. Let cool for 20 minutes. Serve with ice cream or whipped cream.

# blood orange loaf cake

MAKES 1 (9X5-INCH) CAKE

*It's amazing how blogging has opened my eyes to so many different foods. Prior to starting my blog, I'd never heard of a blood orange, but when I saw that beautiful, deep crimson color, I knew I had to get my hands on some to experiment with. When I put them in this loaf, it created such a bright flavor, almost like eating a ray of sunshine. The moist loaf is drizzled in a zingy glaze that will make you want to dunk the whole slice in it.*

**CAKE:**
- 2¼ cups (281 grams) all-purpose flour
- 1 teaspoon (5 grams) baking powder
- ½ teaspoon (1.5 grams) kosher salt
- 1 cup (200 grams) granulated sugar
- 3 tablespoons (18 grams) blood orange zest
- 2 tablespoons (28 grams) firmly packed light brown sugar
- ½ cup (113 grams) unsalted butter, melted
- ¼ cup (56 grams) vegetable oil
- 3 large eggs (150 grams), room temperature
- ½ cup (120 grams) fresh blood orange juice
- ½ teaspoon (2 grams) vanilla extract
- ½ teaspoon (2 grams) orange extract

**GLAZE:**
- 1½ cups (180 grams) confectioners' sugar
- 3 tablespoons (45 grams) fresh blood orange juice
- 1 tablespoon (15 grams) heavy whipping cream

1. Preheat oven to 350°F (180°C). Using a pastry brush, brush a 9x5-inch loaf pan with Cake Release (recipe on page 31) or spray with baking spray with flour.
2. For the cake: In a medium bowl, whisk together flour, baking powder, and salt.
3. In a medium bowl, pinch together granulated sugar, blood orange zest, and brown sugar until fragrant. Add melted butter and oil. Whisk until well combined. Add eggs, one at a time, ensuring each egg is fully incorporated prior to adding the next, about 15 seconds each. Add blood orange juice and extracts. Whisk until combined. Gradually add flour mixture, whisking until just combined. Pour into prepared pan.
4. Bake until golden brown and a wooden pick inserted in center comes out with only a few moist crumbs, about 1 hour and 20 minutes. Let cool in pan for 5 minutes. Remove from pan, and let cool completely on a wire rack.
5. For the glaze: In a medium bowl, whisk together all ingredients. Drizzle glaze onto cooled cake.

# mile-high cherry meringue tart

**MAKES 1 (9½-INCH) TART**

*Get ready to raise your dessert experience to impressive heights. The graham cracker tart shell is filled to the brim with a rich cherry curd filling, bursting with sweet and tart flavors. It's then topped with a towering cloud of fluffy meringue, toasted to perfection!*

CRUST:
- 10 graham cracker sheets (about 150 grams)
- 3 tablespoons (36 grams) granulated sugar
- Pinch kosher salt
- 7 tablespoons (98 grams) unsalted butter, melted

FILLING:
- 1 pound (453 grams) pitted fresh cherries
- ½ cup (100 grams) granulated sugar
- 1 tablespoon (15 grams) fresh lemon juice
- 2 tablespoons (30 grams) water
- 1 tablespoon (8 grams) cornstarch
- 1 tablespoon (14 grams) unsalted butter
- ½ teaspoon (2 grams) almond extract

MERINGUE:
- 1 tablespoon (15 grams) lemon juice
- 4 large egg whites (120 grams)
- ¾ cup (150 grams) granulated sugar
- ½ teaspoon (2.5 grams) cream of tartar

1. Preheat oven to 350°F (180°C).
2. For the crust: In the bowl of a food processor, process graham crackers, sugar, and salt until fine, uniform crumbs form. With food processor running, add melted butter. Scrape down sides of bowl. Continue to process until texture resembles wet sand. Using the bottom of a cup, press mixture into bottom and up sides of a 9½-inch round fluted tart pan with removable bottom.
3. Bake until set and fragrant, 20 to 25 minutes.
4. For the filling: In a medium saucepan, combine cherries, sugar, and lemon juice. Cook, stirring frequently, until mixture comes to a boil and cherries begin to burst, about 10 minutes.
5. Carefully pour hot cherry mixture into the container of a blender, and process until smooth. Return mixture to saucepan.
6. In a small bowl, stir together 2 tablespoons (30 grams) water and cornstarch. Pour cornstarch slurry into cherry mixture, and stir until well combined. Cook over medium heat, stirring constantly, until mixture thickens and cornstarch flavor is cooked out, about 5 minutes. Stir in butter and almond extract, and remove from heat. Pour into prepared crust. Cover with plastic wrap, pressing wrap directly onto surface of filling to prevent a film from forming. Let cool at room temperature for 1 hour; refrigerate until fully set, at least 4 hours.
7. For the meringue: In the bowl of a stand mixer, place lemon juice. Using a paper towel, wipe down sides and bottom of bowl with lemon juice until nothing remains. (This will help remove any oils and excess moisture from the bowl.) Let dry.
8. In the top of a double boiler, whisk together egg whites and sugar. Cook over simmering water, stirring frequently, until sugar fully dissolves and an instant-read thermometer registers 150°F (65°C). (Sugar is dissolved when you can rub the mixture between your fingers and feel no sugar.)
9. Transfer egg white mixture to the cleaned bowl of a stand mixer fitted with the whisk attachment. Add cream of tartar, and beat on low speed, increasing mixer speed to medium as mixture becomes bubbly. Beat until stiff peaks form and meringue is glossy and white, 7 to 10 minutes. Spoon meringue onto tart. Using a handheld kitchen torch, carefully brown meringue.

# lemon-raspberry swiss roll

MAKES 1 SWISS ROLL

*The citrus notes in this light and airy cake encircle a tart raspberry filling for a truly sensational combo. You won't be able to stop at just one bite.*

CAKE:
- 1¾ cups (219 grams) cake flour
- 1 teaspoon (5 grams) baking powder
- ¼ teaspoon kosher salt
- 5 large eggs (250 grams), separated and room temperature
- ¼ teaspoon cream of tartar
- ½ cup plus 4 tablespoons (148 grams) granulated sugar, divided
- ½ cup (112 grams) vegetable oil
- ½ cup (120 grams) whole milk
- 1 tablespoon (13 grams) lemon extract

Confectioners' sugar, for dusting

FILLING:
- 1 (8-ounce) package (226 grams) cream cheese, softened
- 1 cup (120 grams) confectioners' sugar
- 1 cup (240 grams) heavy whipping cream
- ¼ cup (80 grams) raspberry preserves

Garnish: fresh raspberries

1. Preheat oven to 325°F (170°C). Line an 18x13-inch rimmed baking sheet with parchment paper.
2. For the cake: In a small bowl, whisk together flour, baking powder, and salt.
3. In the bowl of a stand mixer fitted with the whisk attachment, beat egg whites and cream of tartar on medium-low speed until bubbly, 1 to 2 minutes. With mixer running, slowly add 3 tablespoons (36 grams) granulated sugar. Increase mixer speed to medium, and beat until stiff peaks form, 5 to 7 minutes.
4. In a large bowl, beat egg yolks and remaining ½ cup plus 1 tablespoon (112 grams) granulated sugar with a handheld mixer on medium speed until bubbly and lighter in color, about 2 minutes. Add oil, and continue to beat until well combined, about 1 minute. Add milk and lemon extract, and continue to beat until well combined, about 1 minute. Gradually add flour mixture alternately with egg white mixture, beginning and ending with flour mixture, folding with a silicone spatula until just combined after each addition. Pour batter into prepared pan. Using an offset spatula, spread smooth. Tap pan on a kitchen towel-lined counter to release excess air bubbles.
5. Bake until a wooden pick inserted in center comes out clean, 20 to 22 minutes. Using a fine-mesh sieve, dust confectioners' sugar on top of cake. Top with a clean kitchen towel and a cutting board. Invert cake onto cutting board. Starting with one short side, roll up cake with towel into a spiral. Let cool completely, 45 minutes to 1 hour.
6. For the filling: In the bowl of a stand mixer fitted with the whisk attachment, beat cream cheese on medium speed until fluffy, about 1 minute. Add confectioners' sugar and cream; continue to beat until smooth, 1 to 2 minutes. Add preserves, and continue to beat until combined.
7. Carefully unroll cooled cake. Using an offset spatula, spread filling into an even layer on cooled cake. Gently reroll cake without towel, tucking tightly without pressing too hard. Refrigerate until set, at least 1 hour.
8. Using a small, fine-mesh strainer, dust with confectioners' sugar. Garnish with raspberries, if desired.

# peach cobbler whoopie pies

**MAKES 16 WHOOPIE PIES**

*Get ready to indulge in a delightful marriage of two beloved desserts. Tasty peaches and a generous dollop of vanilla frosting are sandwiched between cake-like cookies for a memorable summer treat.*

**FILLING:**
- 1½ pounds (680 grams) fresh peaches, diced
- ¾ cup (165 grams) firmly packed light brown sugar
- ½ cup (100 grams) granulated sugar
- 1 teaspoon (2 grams) ground cinnamon
- 1 teaspoon (5 grams) fresh lemon juice
- ¼ teaspoon ground nutmeg
- Pinch kosher salt
- 1 tablespoon (8 grams) cornstarch

**COOKIES:**
- 3 cups plus 2 tablespoons (391 grams) all-purpose flour
- 2 teaspoons (4 grams) ground cinnamon
- 1 teaspoon (5 grams) baking powder
- ½ teaspoon (2.5 grams) baking soda
- ½ teaspoon (1.5 grams) kosher salt
- ½ cup (113 grams) unsalted butter, room temperature
- ¾ cup (165 grams) firmly packed light brown sugar
- ½ cup (100 grams) granulated sugar
- 2 tablespoons (28 grams) vegetable oil
- 2 large eggs (100 grams), room temperature
- 1½ teaspoons (6 grams) vanilla extract
- ½ cup (120 grams) sour cream, room temperature
- ½ cup (120 grams) whole milk, room temperature

**BUTTERCREAM:**
- ¾ cup (170 grams) unsalted butter, room temperature
- 3 cups (360 grams) confectioners' sugar
- 2 tablespoons (30 grams) whole milk
- 1½ teaspoons (6 grams) vanilla extract
- ⅛ teaspoon kosher salt

**1.** For the filling: In a medium saucepan, cook peaches, brown sugar, granulated sugar, cinnamon, lemon juice, nutmeg, and salt over medium heat, stirring occasionally, until juices bubble and peaches begin to soften, about 10 minutes.

**2.** In a small bowl, place cornstarch; add 2 tablespoons (30 grams) liquid from peach mixture, and whisk until combined. Stir cornstarch slurry into peach mixture, and continue to cook, stirring constantly, until mixture begins to thicken. Remove from heat, and let cool to room temperature.

**3.** Preheat oven to 350°F (180°C). Line 2 baking sheets with parchment paper.

**4.** For the cookies: In a medium bowl, whisk together flour, cinnamon, baking powder, baking soda, and salt.

**5.** In the bowl of a stand mixer fitted with the paddle attachment, beat butter, brown sugar, granulated sugar, and oil on medium speed until fluffy, about 5 minutes, scraping down sides of bowl halfway through mixing. Add eggs, one at a time, ensuring each egg is fully incorporated prior to adding the next. Beat in vanilla extract.

**6.** In a small bowl, whisk together sour cream and milk. With mixer on low speed, gradually add sour cream mixture alternately with flour mixture, beginning with sour cream mixture and ending with flour mixture, beating until just combined and scraping down sides of bowl after each addition. (Batter may split after adding the sour cream mixture, but it will come back together as the dry ingredients are added.) Using a 2-tablespoon spring-loaded scoop, scoop dough (about 28 grams each), and place 2 inches apart onto prepared pans.

**7.** Bake, one pan at a time, until edges are set and centers are puffy, 9 to 11 minutes. Let cool on pans for 5 minutes. Remove from pans, and let cool completely on a wire rack.

**8.** For the buttercream: In the bowl of a stand mixer fitted with the paddle attachment, beat butter on medium speed until smooth and fluffy, about 3 minutes. Add confectioners' sugar, and slowly increase mixer speed to medium, beating until well combined. Add milk, vanilla extract, and salt, and beat on high speed until light and fluffy, about 2 minutes. Place buttercream in a pastry bag fitted with your favorite piping tip.

**9.** Pair up cookies so they are similar in shape and size. Pipe buttercream around outside edge on flat side of half of cookies. Place 1 tablespoon (24 grams) filling within each buttercream border. Place remaining cookies, flat side down, on top.

# berrylicious four-berry crisp

MAKES 12 SERVINGS

*Picture a medley of juicy ripe raspberries, plump blueberries, succulent blackberries, and sweet strawberries all together in one beautiful pan, baked until the oat topping is crisp. As the berries bake in the oven, they become caramelized, giving way to a jammy, slightly tart celebration of flavor.*

TOPPING:
- 1 cup (125 grams) all-purpose flour
- ¾ cup (165 grams) firmly packed light brown sugar
- ½ teaspoon (1 gram) ground cinnamon
- ½ cup (113 grams) cold unsalted butter, cubed
- 1 cup (100 grams) old-fashioned oats
- Pinch kosher salt

FILLING:
- 1 pound (454 grams) fresh strawberries, trimmed and halved
- 2 cups (300 grams) fresh blueberries
- 1½ cups (258 grams) fresh blackberries
- 1½ cups (250 grams) fresh raspberries
- ⅔ cup (133 grams) granulated sugar
- 3 tablespoons (24 grams) cornstarch
- 3 tablespoons (60 grams) raspberry preserves
- 1 teaspoon (5 grams) fresh lemon juice

Vanilla ice cream or whipped cream, to serve

**1.** Preheat oven to 350°F (180°C).
**2.** In a medium bowl, stir together flour, brown sugar, and cinnamon. Using your fingertips, cut in cold butter until pea-size pieces remain. Using your hands, mix in oats and salt. Cover and refrigerate until butter is set, 20 to 30 minutes.
**3.** For the filling: In a large bowl, toss together all ingredients, ensuring berries are fully coated. Let stand for 10 minutes.
**4.** Transfer filling to 12-inch cast-iron skillet. Sprinkle topping onto filling.
**5.** Bake until filling is bubbling and topping is golden brown, 45 minutes to 1 hour. Let cool for 20 minutes. Serve warm with ice cream or whipped cream.

# banana pudding pavlova

### MAKES 8 SERVINGS

*Banana pudding on its own is incredible, but when you pour it on top of a crunchy, sweet Pavlova and top it with butter cookies? Words don't do this recipe justice. Use the cookies as a spoon to scoop up all of the delicious pudding and the Pavlova in one bite. It's sheer bliss.*

MERINGUE:
- 1 tablespoon (15 grams) fresh lemon juice
- 6 large egg whites (180 grams)
- 1 cup (200 grams) granulated sugar
- ½ teaspoon cream of tartar
- 2 teaspoons (12 grams) vanilla bean paste

PUDDING:
- Pastry Cream with Banana Milk Alternative (recipe on page 30)
- ¼ cup (60 grams) whole milk

WHIPPED CREAM:
- 1 cup (240 grams) cold heavy whipping cream
- 2 tablespoons (14 grams) confectioners' sugar
- ¼ teaspoon (1 gram) vanilla extract

- 2 medium bananas (227 grams), sliced
- 10 butter cookies (87 grams)

**1.** Preheat oven to 275°F (140°C).

**2.** For the meringue: In the bowl of a stand mixer, place lemon juice. Using a paper towel, wipe down sides and bottom of bowl with lemon juice until nothing remains. (This will help remove any oils and excess moisture from the bowl.) Let dry.

**3.** In the top of a double boiler, whisk together egg whites and granulated sugar. Cook over simmering water, whisking frequently, until sugar fully dissolves and an instant-read thermometer registers 150°F (65°C). (Sugar is dissolved when you can rub the mixture between your fingers and feel no sugar.)

**4.** Transfer egg white mixture to the cleaned bowl of a stand mixer fitted with the whisk attachment. Add cream of tartar, and beat on low speed, increasing mixer speed to medium as mixture becomes bubbly. Beat until stiff peaks form and meringue is glossy and white, 7 to 10 minutes. Add vanilla bean paste, and continue to beat until just combined.

**5.** Draw an 8-inch circle on a piece of parchment paper. Dab a small amount of meringue onto corners of an 18x13-inch baking pan. Place parchment, circle side down, on prepared pan, and press corners of parchment on top of meringue. (This is to prevent the parchment from moving.) Spoon meringue into center of circle, and using a silicone spatula, shape meringue and fill circle. Using a spoon, create an indentation in center of meringue circle so it looks like a bowl. Place in oven.

**6.** Immediately reduce oven temperature to 225°F (107°C), and bake until dry and firm on outside and no longer glossy, about 1½ hours. Turn oven off, and let meringue cool in oven with the door closed overnight.

**7.** For the pudding: Place prepared Pastry Cream with Banana Milk Alternative in a medium bowl, and whisk until smooth. Add milk, and whisk until smooth.

**8.** For the whipped cream: In a large bowl, beat all ingredients with a handheld mixer on medium-high speed until stiff peaks form, 4 to 5 minutes.

**9.** Spoon pudding in center of meringue. Top with whipped cream, sliced bananas, and cookies.

# coconut cornbread cake
## WITH LIME FROSTING

**MAKES 1 (9-INCH) CAKE**

*When you want to go on vacation but can't get away, make this recipe. With each slice, you're transported to a sun-drenched beach, where coconut and lime dance on your palate, evoking feelings of warmth and relaxation with this irresistible tropical combination.*

**CAKE:**
- 1½ cups (188 grams) all-purpose flour
- 1 cup (150 grams) fine yellow cornmeal
- ½ cup (42 grams) sweetened flaked coconut
- 2 teaspoons (10 grams) baking powder
- ½ teaspoon (1.5 grams) kosher salt
- ½ cup (110 grams) firmly packed light brown sugar
- ½ cup (113 grams) unsalted butter, melted
- ½ cup (112 grams) vegetable oil
- ⅓ cup (67 grams) granulated sugar
- 2 large eggs (100 grams), room temperature
- 1 cup (240 grams) whole buttermilk, room temperature
- ½ cup (120 grams) cream of coconut
- 2 teaspoons (8 grams) coconut extract
- 1 teaspoon (4 grams) vanilla extract

**FROSTING:**
- 4 ounces (113 grams) cream cheese, softened
- ¼ cup (57 grams) unsalted butter, room temperature
- 2 cups (240 grams) confectioners' sugar
- 1 tablespoon (6 grams) lime zest
- 2 tablespoons (30 grams) fresh lime juice
- 1 to 2 tablespoons (15 to 30 grams) heavy whipping cream

Garnish: sweetened flaked coconut, lime slices

1. Preheat oven to 400°F (200°C). Spray a 9-inch round cake pan with baking spray with flour.
2. For the cake: In a medium bowl, whisk together flour, cornmeal, flaked coconut, baking powder, and salt.
3. In a large bowl, beat brown sugar, melted butter, oil, granulated sugar, and eggs with a handheld mixer on medium speed until well combined. Add buttermilk, cream of coconut, and extracts, and continue to beat until fully combined. Add flour mixture, and continue to beat until combined. Spread batter into prepared pan.
4. Bake until a wooden pick inserted in center comes out clean, 30 to 35 minutes. Let cool in pan for 10 minutes. Remove from pan, and let cool completely on a wire rack.
5. For the frosting: In a large bowl, beat cream cheese and butter with a handheld mixer on medium speed until creamy, about 1 minute. Add confectioners' sugar, lime zest and juice, and 1 tablespoon (15 grams) cream, and continue to beat until smooth. (If frosting is too thick, add up to 1 tablespoon (15 grams) cream and beat until smooth.) Spread frosting on top of cooled cake. Garnish with flaked coconut and lime slices, if desired.

# fresh peach olive oil cake

MAKES 1 (9-INCH) CAKE

*Emphasize the vibrancy of summer with this moist cake infused with the delicate sweetness of ripe peaches and the subtle earthiness of olive oil. With each bite, you'll experience the perfect balance of richness, lightened by the floral aroma of fresh peaches.*

TOPPING:
- 1 pound fresh peaches (454 grams), peeled and sliced
- ¼ cup (55 grams) firmly packed light brown sugar
- 1 tablespoon (15 grams) fresh lemon juice
- 1 teaspoon (2 grams) ground cinnamon
- ¼ teaspoon ground ginger
- ¼ teaspoon ground nutmeg

CAKE:
- 1 cup (200 grams) granulated sugar
- ½ cup (110 grams) firmly packed light brown sugar
- ½ cup (112 grams) extra-virgin olive oil
- 3 large eggs (150 grams), room temperature
- ½ cup (120 grams) sour cream, room temperature
- 1½ teaspoons (6 grams) vanilla extract
- 1 teaspoon (4 grams) almond extract
- 2¼ cups (281 grams) all-purpose flour
- 1 teaspoon (5 grams) baking powder
- 1 teaspoon (3 grams) kosher salt
- 1 teaspoon (2 grams) ground cinnamon
- ½ teaspoon (2.5 grams) baking soda
- ½ teaspoon (1 gram) ground ginger
- ¼ teaspoon ground nutmeg

- 1 tablespoon (20 grams) apricot preserves

Confectioners' sugar, for dusting

1. Preheat oven to 350°F (180°C). Spray a 9-inch springform pan with baking spray with flour.
2. For the topping: In a large bowl, toss together peaches, brown sugar, lemon juice, cinnamon, ginger, and nutmeg. Let stand for 20 minutes.
3. For the cake: In another large bowl, whisk together granulated sugar, brown sugar, oil, and eggs until well combined. Whisk in sour cream and extracts until well combined. Add flour, baking powder, salt, cinnamon, baking soda, ginger, and nutmeg. Whisk until just combined; pour into prepared pan. Gently place peaches from topping on batter. (Reserve the peach liquid.)
4. Bake until a wooden pick inserted in center comes out clean, 1 hour and 10 minutes to 1 hour and 20 minutes. Let cool in pan for 20 minutes. Remove from pan, and place on a wire rack.
5. In a small microwave-safe bowl, whisk together reserved peach liquid and preserves. Microwave just until preserves are fully melted, 20 to 40 seconds. Brush on top of cake. Dust with confectioners' sugar. Serve warm or at room temperature.

# candied grapefruit macarons

MAKES ABOUT 20 MACARONS

*The bitter bite of grapefruit pastry cream is balanced by the sweet crunch of macaron shells. Topped with candied grapefruit peels, these macarons are truly enjoyable, start to finish.*

CANDIED GRAPEFRUIT PEEL:
Peel of ½ large grapefruit (40 grams), cut into ⅛-inch slices (See Pro Tip)
1½ cups (300 grams) granulated sugar, divided

MACARON SHELLS:
2 cups (240 grams) confectioners' sugar
1¼ cups (120 grams) superfine almond flour
1 tablespoon (15 grams) fresh lemon juice
½ cup plus 5 teaspoons (120 grams) granulated sugar
Scant 9 tablespoons (130 grams) egg whites (4 to 5 large egg whites)
½ teaspoon (1 gram) cream of tartar
1 teaspoon (4 grams) vanilla extract

FILLING:
Pastry Cream (recipe on page 30)
2 tablespoons (12 grams) grapefruit zest
6 tablespoons (90 grams) fresh grapefruit juice
Pink gel food coloring

**PRO TIP:** *To ensure your dessert isn't bitter, remove the white pith from the grapefruit peels.*

1. For the candied grapefruit peel: In a small saucepan, add grapefruit peels and enough water to just cover. Bring to a boil, and boil for 5 minutes; drain. Repeat once. Add enough water to cover peels, and add 1 cup (200 grams) granulated sugar. Bring to a boil; reduce heat, and simmer until mixture is syrupy, 15 to 20 minutes. Remove from heat, and let stand for 10 minutes. Drain peels, and toss in remaining ½ cup (100 grams) granulated sugar. Store, covered in granulated sugar, in an airtight container until ready to use.
2. For the macaron shells: Line 3 rimmed baking sheets with a 2-inch macaron silicone baking mats.
3. In the bowl of a food processor, process confectioners' sugar and almond flour until well combined, about 30 seconds. Sift twice into a large bowl.
4. In the bowl of a stand mixer, place lemon juice. Using a paper towel, wipe down sides and bottom of bowl with lemon juice until nothing remains. Let dry.
5. In the top of a double boiler, whisk together granulated sugar, egg whites, and cream of tartar. Cook over simmering water, whisking frequently, until sugar fully dissolves and an instant-read thermometer registers 150°F (65°C).
6. Transfer egg white mixture to the cleaned bowl of a stand mixer fitted with the whisk attachment. Beat on low speed, increasing mixer speed to medium as mixture becomes bubbly. Beat until stiff peaks form and meringue is glossy and white, 7 to 10 minutes. Add vanilla extract, beating until just combined. Using a silicone spatula, gradually fold in flour mixture until fully combined. Continue folding until batter is smooth and flows like lava. The batter is ready once you can move the spatula over the batter in a figure eight motion and the batter does not break.
7. Transfer batter to a pastry bag fitted with a ½-inch round piping tip. Holding piping tip perpendicularly to a prepared pan, pipe batter onto circles on silicone mat. Firmly tap pan vigorously on counter 5 to 7 times to release air bubbles. Repeat with remaining batter on remaining pans. If any bubbles do not pop, use a

wooden pick to pop bubbles. Let stand at room temperature until a skin forms and they are no longer shiny, 35 minutes to 45 minutes. (This process may take longer if your home is more humid.)

**8.** Preheat oven to 300°F (150°C).

**9.** Bake, one pan at a time, until macaron shells form a bubbly bottom edge, 16 to 18 minutes. (When touched, the macaron shells should not move around.) Let cool completely on pans.

**10.** For the filling: Place prepared Pastry Cream in medium bowl, and whisk until smooth. Add grapefruit zest and juice, and whisk until just combined. Whisk in food coloring to desired shade just until combined.

**11.** Transfer filling to a pastry bag fitted with your favorite piping tip. Pipe filling onto flat side of half of cooled macaron shells. Gently place remaining macaron shells, flat side down, on top of filling. Pipe a small dollop of filling on top of each macaron. Top with candied grapefruit peel.

FRUITY AND FABULOUS

# coconut cake
## WITH PASSION FRUIT CURD

MAKES 1 (9-INCH) CAKE

*Coconut cake is so underrated with its soft texture. Layered with a lush passion fruit curd filling, this cake tastes like a day on the beach, letting the sun kiss your skin!*

PASSION FRUIT CURD:
- 5 large egg yolks (95 grams)
- ½ cup (100 grams) granulated sugar
- ½ cup (120 grams) passion fruit juice
- Pinch kosher salt
- 1 tablespoon (14 grams) unsalted butter
- 1 tablespoon (15 grams) fresh lime juice

CAKE:
- 3 cups (375 grams) cake flour
- 2¼ cups (450 grams) granulated sugar
- ¾ cup (63 grams) sweetened flaked coconut
- ½ cup (113 grams) salted butter, cubed and room temperature
- 1 tablespoon (15 grams) baking powder
- 1 teaspoon (3 grams) kosher salt
- 1 cup (240 grams) full-fat coconut milk
- ½ cup (112 grams) vegetable oil
- ½ cup (120 grams) sour cream, room temperature
- 3 large eggs (150 grams), room temperature
- 2 large egg whites (60 grams), room temperature
- 2 tablespoons (30 grams) cream of coconut
- 1 teaspoon (4 grams) vanilla extract

Swiss Meringue Buttercream (recipe on page 27)
- 2 cups (160 grams) sweetened flaked coconut, for coating

**1.** For the passion fruit curd: In the top of a double boiler, whisk together egg yolks, sugar, passion fruit juice, and salt. Cook over simmering water, whisking constantly, until mixture begins to thicken, 3 to 5 minutes. Remove from heat, and whisk in butter and lime juice until butter is melted and fully incorporated. Place in a heatproof bowl, and cover with plastic wrap, pressing wrap directly onto surface of curd to prevent a film from forming. Refrigerate until fully set, 1 to 2 hours.

**2.** Preheat oven to 350°F (180°C). Using a pastry brush, brush 3 (8-inch) round cake pans with Cake Release (recipe on page 31) or spray with baking spray with flour.

**3.** For the cake: In the bowl of a stand mixer fitted with the paddle attachment, beat flour, sugar, flaked coconut, butter, baking powder, and salt on medium speed until mixture has a sandy texture and butter is fully incorporated, 1 to 2 minutes.

**4.** In a medium bowl, whisk together coconut milk, oil, sour cream, eggs, egg whites, cream of coconut, and vanilla extract until smooth. Add coconut milk mixture to flour mixture, and beat on medium speed for 2 minutes, scraping down sides of bowl. Divide batter among prepared pans.

**5.** Bake until a wooden pick inserted in center comes out clean, 35 to 40 minutes. Let cool in pans completely on wire racks.

**6.** Add about 1½ cups Swiss Meringue Buttercream to a pastry bag, and cut a 1-inch opening in tip.

**7.** Remove cooled cakes from pans, and spread a thin layer of Swiss Meringue Buttercream on top of 2 cake layers, and place 1 coated cake layer on a cake stand. Pipe buttercream around perimeter of cake layer and then spread half of passion fruit curd inside buttercream border. Place second coated cake layer on top. Repeat with other prepared cake layer. Top with remaining cake layer, and cover with a thin layer of buttercream. Refrigerate for 30 minutes.

**8.** Spread remaining buttercream on top and sides of cake, and coat with flaked coconut.

# a little something savory

# asiago-and-thyme cheese puffs

MAKES ABOUT 24 PUFFS

*These bite-size wonders are bursting with the savory goodness of sharp Asiago cheese and fragrant thyme. With a delightful crunch on the outside as the cheesy center melts in your mouth, make sure to grab a handful because these will be gone before you know it!*

- ¾ cup (180 grams) whole milk
- ½ cup (113 grams) unsalted butter
- ¼ cup (60 grams) water
- 1¼ cups (156 grams) all-purpose flour
- 2 tablespoons (3 grams) fresh thyme leaves
- ½ teaspoon (1.5 grams) kosher salt
- ¼ teaspoon ground black pepper
- ⅛ teaspoon ground nutmeg
- 8 ounces (226 grams) shredded Asiago cheese
- 4 large eggs (200 grams), room temperature
- Flaked sea salt, to taste

**1.** Preheat oven to 425°F (220°C). Line 2 rimmed baking sheets with parchment paper.

**2.** In a medium saucepan, bring milk, butter, and ¼ cup (60 grams) water to a boil over medium heat. Add flour, thyme, kosher salt, pepper, and nutmeg. Using a wooden spoon, stir until a dough forms. Continue to stir until a film forms on bottom of pan, about 2 minutes.

**3.** Transfer dough to the bowl of a stand mixer fitted with the paddle attachment. Beat on low speed until dough has cooled but is still warm to the touch, 2 to 3 minutes. Add 6 ounces (170 grams) cheese, and continue to beat until combined, 20 to 30 seconds. Add eggs, one at a time, ensuring each egg is fully incorporated prior to adding the next, about 15 seconds each. Increase mixer speed to medium-high, and beat until dough forms a ball, 3 to 5 minutes. Transfer batter to a 12-inch pastry bag fitted with a ½-inch round piping tip. Pipe circles 2 inches apart on prepared pan. (Each puff should be about 2 tablespoons batter.) Sprinkle with remaining 2 ounces (56 grams) cheese.

**4.** Bake until puffed and golden brown, 17 to 18 minutes. Sprinkle with sea salt to taste.

# fig, prosciutto, rosemary, and olive focaccia

MAKES 1 (13X9-INCH) LOAF

*This recipe was inspired by my travels to Portofino, Italy, with* Bake from Scratch *magazine when I was about seven months pregnant. Me and my big bump ate everything in sight, but my favorite thing was focaccia. This artisanal bread boasts a stunning texture, generously studded with plump figs, briny olives, fragrant rosemary, and thinly sliced prosciutto. Every time I make this, it takes me right back to that place.*

DOUGH:
- 3 cups (720 grams) warm water (105°F/41°C to 110°F/43°C)
- 1 tablespoon (9 grams) active dry yeast
- 1 teaspoon (4 grams) granulated sugar
- 6¼ cups (794 grams) bread flour
- 2 tablespoons (28 grams) olive oil, plus more for oiling pan and hands
- 4 teaspoons (12 grams) kosher salt

TOPPING:
- 8 fresh figs (80 grams), cut into quarters
- 4 slices prosciutto (50 grams), cut into 1-inch squares
- 4 sprigs fresh rosemary
- ¼ cup (55 grams) sliced black olives
- 1 to 2 tablespoons (14 to 28 grams) olive oil
- Flaked sea salt, to taste

**1.** For the dough: In a large bowl, whisk together 3 cups (720 grams) warm water, yeast, and sugar. Let stand until bloomed and foaming, 5 to 10 minutes.

**2.** Add flour, oil, and kosher salt to yeast mixture. Using your hands, mix together until fully combined and a dough forms. Cover, and let rest until dough is very bubbly and risen, about 1 hour.

**3.** Slightly punch down dough. Stretch one side of dough upward and fold over to opposite side of dough; rotate bowl. Repeat stretching and folding process 3 times, rotating bowl after each fold. Cover dough, and let rest for 30 minutes. Repeat folding process 2 more times, letting rest between each set of folds. After the final fold, cover with plastic wrap, and refrigerate for 4 hours.

**4.** Punch down dough. Stretch and fold 4 times, rotating bowl between each fold. Cover and refrigerate dough to cold-ferment for at least 8 hours or up to overnight. (See note.)

**5.** Before you're ready to bake, press dough into a well-oiled 13x9-inch rimmed baking sheet. Cover and let rest at room temperature for 2 hours.

**6.** Preheat oven to 400°F (200°C).

**7.** For the topping: In a large bowl, combine figs, prosciutto, rosemary, and olives. Drizzle with 1 to 2 tablespoons (14 to 28 grams) oil, and toss to coat. (This will prevent toppings from burning in the oven.)

**8.** Cover your hands in oil, and press your fingertips into dough to create dimples or indentations at 1-inch intervals. Place topping on dough. Sprinkle with sea salt.

**9.** Bake until golden brown, 35 to 40 minutes.

NOTE: *Cold-fermenting dough involves allowing the dough to rise slowly in the refrigerator instead of at room temperature. This extended fermentation period enhances the flavor and texture of the bread, resulting in a more complex taste and lighter crumb.*

# black pepper-and-gruyère popovers

MAKES 6 POPOVERS

*The nutty flavor of Gruyère and the fruity notes of black pepper make these beautifully crisp popovers a tantalizing addition to any meal.*

- 1¼ cups (156 grams) all-purpose flour
- 3 ounces (85 grams) Gruyère cheese, shredded
- ¾ teaspoon (1.5 grams) ground black pepper
- ½ teaspoon (1.5 grams) kosher salt
- ½ teaspoon chopped fresh rosemary
- ⅛ teaspoon ground nutmeg
- 1¼ cups (300 grams) whole milk
- 2 large eggs (100 grams)
- 6 teaspoons (30 grams) salted butter, divided

**1.** Position oven rack to second-to-bottom shelf. Preheat oven to 450°F (230°C). Place a 6-cup popover pan on oven rack in preheating oven.

**2.** In a medium bowl, whisk together flour, cheese, pepper, salt, rosemary, and nutmeg.

**3.** In another medium bowl, beat milk and eggs with a handheld mixer on high speed for 3 minutes. Add flour mixture, and beat until combined.

**4.** Carefully remove popover pan from oven. Add 1 teaspoon (5 grams) butter to each cup, and let melt. Once melted, use a pastry brush to spread butter all over cup. Add ⅓ cup (123 grams) batter to each prepared cup.

**5.** Bake for 20 minutes. Reduce oven temperature to 350°F (180°C), and bake until tops are golden brown, 10 to 15 minutes more. Let cool in pan for 5 minutes.

# sage, browned butter, and parmesan biscotti

MAKES ABOUT 36 BISCOTTI

*Fragrant sage leaves add a burst of herbal freshness while sharp Parmesan cheese provides a savory punch that balances the nutty richness of browned butter.*

| | |
|---|---|
| 2 | cups (250 grams) all-purpose flour |
| 1 | cup (100 grams) freshly grated Parmesan cheese |
| 1 | teaspoon (5 grams) baking powder |
| 1 | teaspoon (3 grams) kosher salt |
| ½ | teaspoon (1 gram) ground sage |
| ½ | teaspoon (1 gram) ground black pepper |
| ¼ | cup (57 grams) unsalted butter |
| 7 | fresh sage leaves, chopped |
| 1 | clove garlic (3 grams), finely diced |
| 4 | large eggs (200 grams), divided |

**1.** Preheat oven to 375°F (190°C). Line a baking sheet with parchment paper.

**2.** In a medium bowl, whisk together flour, Parmesan, baking powder, salt, ground sage, and pepper.

**3.** In a small saucepan, melt butter over medium-low heat. Add sage leaves, and cook, stirring occasionally, until browned and foamy. (Browned bits should appear on bottom of pan underneath foam, and the color should be a deep golden brown.) Remove from heat, and stir in garlic. Let cool 5 to 10 minutes.

**4.** In a large bowl, whisk 3 eggs (150 grams) until fluffy, about 3 minutes. Whisk in sage browned butter until well combined. Fold in flour mixture until a dough forms. Divide dough in half (about 275 grams each). Place on prepared pan, and using wet hands, shape each half into a 10x3-inch log, spacing about 2 inches apart.

**5.** In a small bowl, whisk remaining 1 egg (50 grams). Using a pastry brush, brush dough with egg.

**6.** Bake until lightly golden and completely dry, about 20 minutes. Let cool on pan for 20 minutes. Leave oven on.

**7.** Using a serrated knife, cut each log crosswise into ½-inch-thick slices. Place, cut side down, on same pan.

**8.** Bake until golden brown and dry, about 15 minutes. Let cool completely on pan.

# browned butter pecan parker house rolls

MAKES 16 ROLLS

*It's hard to improve on the perfection that is browned butter, but when you combine it with pecans in a fluffy roll, it can't be beat. I love to eat these rolls fresh out of the oven with some flaked salt on top.*

ROLLS:
- 1 cup (240 grams) warm whole milk (110°F/43°C to 115°F/46°C)
- 3 tablespoons (36 grams) granulated sugar, divided
- 1 tablespoon (9 grams) active dry yeast
- 4 cups (500 grams) all-purpose flour, plus more for dusting
- ¾ cup (85 grams) chopped pecans
- 1½ teaspoons (4.5 grams) kosher salt
- 6 tablespoons (84 grams) Browned Butter (recipe on page 28), melted and cooled slightly
- 1 large egg (50 grams), room temperature
- 2 large egg yolks (38 grams), room temperature
- 2 tablespoons (28 grams) unsalted butter, room temperature

EGG WASH:
- 1 large egg (50 grams)
- 1 tablespoon (15 grams) water

TOPPING:
- 2 tablespoons (26 grams) Browned Butter (recipe on page 28), melted and cooled slightly
- Flaked sea salt, to taste

1. For the rolls: In a medium bowl, whisk together warm milk, 1 tablespoon (12 grams) sugar, and yeast. Let stand until bloomed and foaming, 5 to 10 minutes.
2. In the bowl of a stand mixer, whisk together flour, pecans, kosher salt, and remaining 2 tablespoons (24 grams) sugar by hand.
3. Whisk melted Browned Butter, egg, and egg yolks into yeast mixture until well combined. Add yeast mixture to flour mixture. Using your hands (or a silicone spatula), mix until a rough dough forms.
4. Fit stand mixer with the dough hook attachment, and knead on medium speed until dough is elastic and pulls away from sides of bowl, about 10 minutes.
5. Place dough in a well-oiled bowl. Cover and let rise in a warm, draft-free place (75°) until doubled in size, about 1 hour.
6. Grease the bottom and sides of a 13x9-inch baking pan with room temperature butter.
7. Punch down dough, and turn out onto a lightly floured surface. Divide dough into 16 equal-size pieces (about 65 grams each). Using your hands, flatten each piece and roll it into a smooth ball. Evenly place in prepared pan in 4 rows of 4. Cover and let rise in a warm, draft-free place (75°F/24°C) until puffy, 40 minutes to 1 hour.
8. Preheat oven to 350°F (180°C).
9. For the egg wash: In a small bowl, whisk together egg and 1 tablespoon (15 grams) water. Using a pastry brush, brush tops of rolls with egg wash.
10. Bake until golden brown, 25 to 30 minutes. Let cool in pan on a wire rack for 5 minutes.
11. For the topping: Brush tops of hot rolls with melted Browned Butter, and sprinkle with sea salt.

# homemade buttermilk biscuits

MAKES ABOUT 6 BISCUITS

*There's something special about a classic buttermilk biscuit, isn't there? Each bite transports you back to simpler times, when mornings were spent gathered around the breakfast table with loved ones. With their golden-brown crust and tender interior, these biscuits symbolize comfort and familiarity, reminding us of the cherished traditions that bind us together. No matter how you eat them, they have a way of warming both the body and the soul.*

- 3½ cups (438 grams) all-purpose flour, plus more for dusting
- 2 tablespoons (24 grams) granulated sugar
- 1 tablespoon (15 grams) baking powder
- 2¼ teaspoons (7 grams) kosher salt
- ½ teaspoon (2.5 grams) baking soda
- 1 cup (227 grams) cold unsalted butter (see note), cubed
- 1 cup (240 grams) cold whole buttermilk
- 2 tablespoons (30 grams) heavy whipping cream

**Melted butter, for brushing**
**Flaked sea salt, to taste**

**1.** Preheat oven to 450°F (230°C). Line a baking sheet with parchment paper.

**2.** In a large bowl, whisk together flour, sugar, baking powder, kosher salt, and baking soda until well combined. Add cold butter. Using your hands, cut butter into flour mixture until butter pieces are pea-size. Add cold buttermilk. Using a wooden spoon, stir until a shaggy dough forms.

**3.** Turn out dough onto a lightly floured surface. Gently pat crumbs into dough until no longer shaggy. Pat or roll dough into a 1-inch-thick rectangle. Using a sharp knife, cut into quarters. Stack quarters on top of each other, and pat down into 1-inch-thick rectangle. Repeat procedure 2 more times, making sure to press back into a 1-inch-thick rectangle each time. Using a rolling pin, roll dough to 1-inch thickness. Using a 2¾-inch round cutter, cut dough without twisting cutter. (Simply press into dough. Otherwise, the biscuits will not rise properly.) Place 1 inch apart on prepared pan. Fold any excess dough back together, and roll to 1-inch thickness. Cut dough, and place on prepared pan. Repeat until no dough remains. Freeze until cold, about 20 minutes.

**4.** Remove biscuits from freezer. Using a pastry brush, brush tops of biscuits with cream.

**5.** Bake until golden brown and flaky layers are visible, 14 to 15 minutes. Brush with melted butter, and sprinkle with sea salt to taste.

**NOTE:** *For extra-cold butter, I like to place mine in the freezer for 20 minutes before I start baking.*

# croissant loaf

**MAKES 1 (9-INCH) LOAF**

*Despite its fancy appearance, this loaf is surprisingly easy to make, requiring just a few basic ingredients and simple techniques. My Croissant Loaf is a deliciously approachable treat that promises to elevate any breakfast or brunch spread with its golden layers.*

## DOUGH:

- 1½ cups (360 grams) warm whole milk (105°F/41°C to 110°F/43°C)
- 3 tablespoons (36 grams) granulated sugar, divided
- 1 tablespoon (9 grams) active dry yeast
- 4¼ cups plus 2 tablespoons (556 grams) bread flour, plus more for dusting
- 2 teaspoons (6 grams) kosher salt
- ½ cup (112 grams) salted butter, room temperature and divided
- 1 cup (227 grams) cold salted butter

## EGG WASH:

- 1 large egg (50 grams)
- 1 tablespoon (15 grams) water

**1.** In a small bowl, gently whisk together warm milk, 1 tablespoon (12 grams) granulated sugar, and yeast. Let stand until bloomed and foaming, 5 to 10 minutes.

**2.** In the bowl of a stand mixer, whisk together flour, salt, and remaining 2 tablespoons (24 grams) sugar. Add yeast mixture, and using a silicone spatula, stir until just combined.

**3.** Fit stand mixer with the dough hook attachment, and knead on low speed for 3 minutes. With mixer on medium-low speed, add ¼ cup (56 grams) room temperature butter, 1 tablespoon (14 grams) at a time, beating until smooth after each addition. (It's OK if the dough breaks when adding the butter; the dough will come back together.)

**4.** Place dough into a well-oiled bowl. Cover and let rise in a warm, draft-free place (75°F/24°C) until doubled in size, 1 to 1½ hours.

**5.** Punch down dough, and turn out onto a lightly floured surface. Roll dough into a 16x12-inch rectangle. Fold one-third of dough over toward center, and place remaining one-third of dough on top, like folding a letter. Unfold dough, and note three sections marked on rectangle.

**6.** Cut cold butter into thin slices, and arrange in center section of dough. Fold dough into letter again to cover butter. Gently press dough with a rolling pin. Turn dough over to back side. Fold in half lengthwise, and wrap in plastic wrap. Refrigerate for 30 minutes.

**7.** Roll dough into a 16x12-inch rectangle. Fold like a letter. Turn dough over, and fold in half lengthwise. Wrap in plastic wrap, and refrigerate for 30 minutes. Repeat procedure one more time.

**8.** Roll dough into a 15x12-inch rectangle, and spread remaining ¼ cup (56 grams) room temperature butter on dough. Starting with one long side, tightly roll up dough into a log, and cut crosswise into 15 1-inch pieces.

**9.** Spray a 9-inch springform pan with baking spray with flour. Place dough pieces in pan, overlapping if necessary to fit. Cover and let rise in a warm, draft-free place (75°F/24°C) until puffy, about 30 minutes.

**10.** Preheat oven to 375°F (190°C). Place a rimmed baking sheet on bottom oven rack. (This will ensure that if any butter leaks from the loaf, it won't end up on the bottom of your oven.)

**11.** For the egg wash: In a small bowl, whisk together egg and 1 tablespoon (15 grams) water. Using a pastry brush, brush tops of rolls with egg wash.

**12.** Bake until deep golden brown, 35 to 40 minutes. Let cool in pan for 30 minutes. Remove from pan, and let cool completely on a wire rack.

# caramelized onion, bacon, and gorgonzola biscuits

MAKES ABOUT 12 BISCUITS

*Caramelized onion and bacon work together to elevate the humble biscuit into a gourmet treat. The pièce de résistance is the creamy and tangy Gorgonzola cheese, which melts into every crumb, infusing the biscuits with its rich and distinctive taste. You get a little sweet, a lot of savory, and a hint of tang with each bite.*

**CARAMELIZED ONION:**
- 2 tablespoons (28 grams) unsalted butter
- 1 tablespoon (14 grams) olive oil
- 1 large yellow onion (170 grams), thinly sliced
- 1 teaspoon (4 grams) granulated sugar
- 2 cups (480 grams) water

**BISCUITS:**
- 2½ cups (313 grams) all-purpose flour, plus more for dusting
- 1 tablespoon (15 grams) baking powder
- 1 teaspoon (1.5 grams) kosher salt
- ¼ teaspoon (1.25 grams) baking soda
- ½ cup (113 grams) cold unsalted butter (see note), cubed
- ½ cup (68 grams) crumbled Gorgonzola cheese
- 4 slices bacon (41 grams), cooked and crumbled
- ½ cup (120 grams) cold whole buttermilk

**EGG WASH:**
- 1 large egg (50 grams)
- 1 tablespoon (15 grams) water

**1.** For the caramelized onion: In a large skillet, melt butter with oil over medium heat. Add onion, and cook, stirring occasionally, until browned, 12 to 15 minutes. Sprinkle with sugar, and cook, stirring frequently, for 2 minutes. Add ½ cup (120 grams) water, and cook, stirring constantly, until water has evaporated, 6 to 8 minutes. Repeat with remaining 1½ cups (360 grams) water, ½ cup (120 grams) at a time, until onions are jammy. Let cool completely. Dice onions.

**2.** Line a rimmed baking sheet with parchment paper.

**3.** For the biscuits: In a large bowl, whisk together flour, baking powder, salt, and baking soda. Add cold butter, tossing to coat. Using your hands, cut butter into flour mixture until butter pieces are pea-size. Using a wooden spoon, mix in caramelized onion, cheese, and bacon. Stir in cold buttermilk until a shaggy dough forms.

**4.** Turn out dough onto a heavily floured surface. Gently pat crumbs into dough until no longer shaggy. Pat dough into a 1-inch-thick rectangle. Using a sharp knife, cut into quarters. Stack quarters on top of each other, and pat down into 1-inch-thick rectangle. Repeat procedure 2 more times, making sure to press back into a 1-inch-thick rectangle each time. Using a rolling pin, roll dough to ½-inch thickness. Using a 2¾-inch round cutter, cut dough without twisting cutter. (Simply press into dough. Otherwise, the biscuits will not rise properly.) Place 2 inches apart on prepared pan. Freeze until cold, about 20 minutes.

**5.** Preheat oven to 450°F (230°C).

**6.** For the egg wash: In a small bowl, whisk together egg and 1 tablespoon (15 grams) water. Using a pastry brush, brush tops of rolls with egg wash.

**7.** Bake until golden brown and tall, 20 to 22 minutes.

**NOTE:** *For extra-cold butter, I like to place mine in the freezer for 20 minutes before I start baking.*

A LITTLE SOMETHING SAVORY

# classic dinner rolls

**MAKES 16 ROLLS**

*Dinner rolls hold a special place in my heart. They're more than just bread—they're a symbol of togetherness and tradition, evoking memories of holiday gatherings and Sunday dinners shared with my loved ones. Every time I eat these rolls, I'm reminded of the love and care that went into creating this recipe, which was passed down through my mom, her mom, and so on. When you break a piece off and slather it with butter, take a second to cherish the timeless ritual of sharing a meal with those you hold dear.*

ROLLS:
- 1 cup (240 grams) warm whole milk (110°F/43°C to 115°/46°C)
- 3½ tablespoons (42 grams) granulated sugar, divided
- 1 tablespoon (9 grams) active dry yeast
- 4½ cups (563 grams) all-purpose flour, plus more for dusting
- 2 teaspoons (6 grams) kosher salt
- ¼ cup (57 grams) unsalted butter, melted and cooled slightly
- 1 large egg (50 grams), room temperature
- 2 large egg yolks (38 grams), room temperature
- 2 tablespoons (28 grams) unsalted butter, room temperature

EGG WASH:
- 1 large egg (50 grams)
- 1 tablespoon (15 grams) water

TOPPING:
- 2 tablespoons (28 grams) unsalted butter, melted
- Flaked sea salt, to taste

**1.** For the rolls: In a medium bowl, whisk together warm milk, 1½ tablespoons (18 grams) sugar, and yeast. Let stand until bloomed and foaming, 5 to 10 minutes.

**2.** In the bowl of a stand mixer, whisk together flour, kosher salt, and remaining 2 tablespoons (24 grams) sugar by hand.

**3.** Whisk melted butter, egg, and egg yolks into yeast mixture until well combined. Add yeast mixture to flour mixture. Using your hands (or a silicone spatula), combine the dry and wet ingredients just until a rough dough forms.

**4.** Fit stand mixer with the dough hook attachment, and knead on medium speed until dough is elastic and pulls from sides of bowl, about 10 minutes.

**5.** Place dough in a well-oiled bowl. Cover and let rise in a warm, draft-free place (75°F/24°C) until doubled in size, 40 minutes to 1 hour.

**6.** Grease the bottom and sides of a 13x9-inch baking pan with room temperature butter.

**7.** Punch down dough, and turn out onto a lightly floured surface. Divide dough into 16 pieces (about 60 grams each). Using your hands, flatten each piece and roll it into a smooth ball. Evenly place into prepared pan in 4 rows of 4. Cover and let rise in a warm, draft-free place (75°F/24°C) until puffy, 40 minutes to 1 hour.

**8.** Preheat oven to 350°F (180°C).

**9.** For the egg wash: In a small bowl, whisk together egg and 1 tablespoon (15 grams) water. Using a pastry brush, brush tops of rolls with egg wash.

**10.** Bake until golden brown, 25 to 30 minutes.

**11.** For topping: Brush tops of rolls with melted butter, and sprinkle with sea salt to taste.

# jalapeño, corn, and oaxaca scones

MAKES ABOUT 9 SCONES

*Are you ready for an epic cheese pull? Oaxaca cheese is creamy and delicious, but when these scones are fresh out of the oven, I love to break one of the scones in half and see the long strings of Oaxaca cheese before enjoying every bite.*

| | |
|---|---|
| 3½ | cups (438 grams) all-purpose flour, plus more for dusting |
| 1½ | tablespoons (22.5 grams) baking powder |
| 2 | teaspoons (6 grams) kosher salt |
| 1 | teaspoon (2 grams) garlic powder |
| 1 | teaspoon (2 grams) dried oregano |
| 1 | teaspoon (2 grams) chili powder |
| ½ | teaspoon (2.5 grams) baking soda |
| ½ | teaspoon (1 gram) ground cumin |
| ⅛ | teaspoon cayenne pepper |
| 1 | cup (227 grams) cold salted butter (see note), cubed |
| 1 | (15-ounce) can (425 grams) yellow corn kernels, drained and patted dry |
| 1 | (8-ounce) package (227 grams) low-moisture Oaxaca cheese, cut into pea-size cubes |
| ½ | cup (70 grams) diced seeded jalapeños (about 2 medium jalapeños) |
| 1 | cup (240 grams) cold whole buttermilk |
| 2 | tablespoons (30 grams) heavy whipping cream |
| 2 | tablespoons (28 grams) salted butter, melted |

Flaked sea salt, to taste

1. Line a baking sheet with parchment paper.
2. In a large bowl, whisk together flour, baking powder, kosher salt, garlic powder, oregano, chili powder, baking soda, cumin, and cayenne pepper. Add cold butter. Using your hands, cut butter into flour mixture until mixture is crumbly and largest butter pieces are pea-size. Using a wooden spoon, stir in corn, cheese, and jalapeños until coated. Add cold buttermilk. Stir until a shaggy dough forms. (Dough may be very crumbly, but do not add more buttermilk!)
3. Turn out dough onto a lightly floured surface. Gently knead dough until it is no longer crumbly. Pat into a 1-inch-thick rectangle. Using a sharp kitchen knife, cut into quarters. Stack quarters on top of each other, and pat down into a 1-inch-thick rectangle. Repeat 2 more times. Pat dough to 1-inch thickness. Using a sharp kitchen knife, cut into 3x2-inch rectangles. Fold together any excess dough, and repeat until all dough is used. Place on prepared pan, and freeze for 20 minutes.
4. Preheat oven to 450°F (230°C).
5. Using a pastry brush, brush scones with cream.
6. Bake until golden brown and flaky layers are visible, 15 to 20 minutes. Brush with melted butter. Sprinkle with sea salt to taste.

NOTE: *For extra-cold butter, I like to place mine in the freezer for 20 minutes before I start baking.*

# nutty necessities

# cardamom and walnut pear crisp

MAKES 8 SERVINGS

*If juicy, tender pears with warm spices beneath a golden crisp topping made with buttery oats and chopped walnuts doesn't immediately make you take notice, I don't know what will! With a scoop of vanilla ice cream, it's heaven in a bowl.*

**TOPPING:**
- ¾ cup (94 grams) all-purpose flour
- ½ cup (110 grams) firmly packed light brown sugar
- ½ teaspoon (1 gram) ground cinnamon
- ¼ teaspoon kosher salt
- ¼ teaspoon ground cardamom
- 6 tablespoons (84 grams) cold unsalted butter, cubed
- ¾ cup (75 grams) old-fashioned oats
- ⅓ cup (38 grams) chopped walnuts

**FILLING:**
- 3 pounds (1,360 grams) firm Bartlett pears, cored and cubed
- ½ cup (100 grams) granulated sugar
- ⅓ cup (38 grams) chopped walnuts
- 1½ tablespoons (12 grams) cornstarch
- 1 tablespoon (6 grams) ground cinnamon
- 1 tablespoon (15 grams) fresh lemon juice
- ½ teaspoon (1.5 grams) kosher salt
- ½ teaspoon (1 gram) ground cardamom
- ¼ teaspoon ground nutmeg

Vanilla ice cream, to serve

1. Preheat oven to 350°F (180°C).
2. For the topping: In a medium bowl, stir together flour, brown sugar, cinnamon, salt, and cardamom. Using your fingertips, cut in cold butter until butter is fully incorporated into mixture. Using your hands, mix in oats and walnuts. Cover and refrigerate until ready to use.
3. For the filling: In a large bowl, stir together all ingredients. Transfer to a 10-inch cast-iron skillet. Sprinkle with topping.
4. Bake until pears are soft (but not mushy) and topping is golden brown, 45 to 50 minutes. Let cool for 10 to 15 minutes. Serve warm with ice cream.

# baklava-stuffed cupcakes
## WITH CINNAMON-ORANGE BUTTERCREAM

**MAKES 12 CUPCAKES**

*In my 33 years on this planet, I have never met a baklava I didn't love, so I wanted to take one of my most beloved desserts and change it up a bit. A vanilla cupcake with a touch of cinnamon is filled with chopped hazelnuts, pistachios, walnuts, honey, sugar, and a little orange zest. Topped with a cinnamon and orange buttercream, this dessert is such a delight.*

CUPCAKES:
- 1½ cups (188 grams) all-purpose flour
- 1 cup (200 grams) granulated sugar
- ½ cup (113 grams) unsalted butter, melted
- 2 tablespoons (28 grams) vegetable oil
- 2 teaspoons (10 grams) baking powder
- ½ teaspoon (1.5 grams) kosher salt
- ½ teaspoon (1 gram) ground cinnamon
- 2 large eggs (100 grams), room temperature
- ½ cup plus 2 tablespoons (150 grams) whole milk, room temperature
- 2 teaspoons (8 grams) vanilla extract

FILLING:
- ⅓ cup (45 grams) walnuts
- 3 tablespoons (30 grams) hazelnuts
- 3 tablespoons (30 grams) pistachios
- 8 teaspoons (56 grams) honey
- 1½ teaspoons (6 grams) granulated sugar
- ½ teaspoon (1 gram) orange zest
- Pinch kosher salt
- Pinch ground cinnamon

BUTTERCREAM:
- ¾ cup (170 grams) unsalted butter, room temperature
- 4 cups (480 grams) confectioners' sugar
- 6 tablespoons (90 grams) heavy whipping cream
- 2 teaspoons (8 grams) vanilla extract
- 1½ teaspoons (3 grams) orange zest
- ¼ teaspoon kosher salt
- ¼ teaspoon ground cinnamon

1. Preheat oven to 350°F (180°C). Line a 12-cup muffin pan with paper liners.
2. For the cupcakes: In a medium bowl, whisk together flour, granulated sugar, melted butter, oil, baking powder, salt, and cinnamon until a thick paste-like batter forms. Add eggs, one at a time, ensuring each egg is fully incorporated prior to adding the next, about 15 seconds each. Add milk and vanilla extract, whisking until just combined. Divide batter among prepared muffin cups, filling each about two-thirds full.
3. Bake until a wooden pick inserted in center comes out clean, about 25 minutes. Let cool completely in pan.
4. For the filling: In the work bowl of a food processor, pulse walnuts, hazelnuts, and pistachios until chopped but not ground, 5 to 10 seconds.
5. In a small bowl, using a silicone spatula, stir together nut mixture, honey, granulated sugar, orange zest, salt, and cinnamon until nuts are fully coated.
6. For the buttercream: In the bowl of a stand mixer fitted with the paddle attachment, beat butter on medium speed for 2 minutes. Add confectioners' sugar, cream, vanilla extract, orange zest, salt, and cinnamon; beat on low speed until fully combined, about 30 seconds. Increase mixer speed to medium, and beat until smooth, about 2 minutes. Scrape down sides and bottom of bowl. Beat on medium-high speed for 1 minute. Transfer buttercream to a large pastry bag fitted with your favorite piping tip.
7. Using a knife, cut a ¾-inch circle in top of each cupcake. Remove circle, and add 2 teaspoons filling to each hole. Using your fingertips, gently press filling into each hole, ensure it's completely full. Top with removed cupcake center. (If the top doesn't fit snugly back into the cupcake, it's OK! The buttercream will cover it.) Pipe buttercream on top of cupcakes. Top with remaining filling.

# cherry-almond cake

MAKES 1 (9-INCH) CAKE

*Fresh cherries meet a buttery cake studded with crunchy almonds, great for pairing with your morning cup of coffee. It's like a warm hug on a lazy weekend morning, with bursts of fruity sweetness and nutty goodness in every bite.*

TOPPING:
- 1 cup (125 grams) all-purpose flour
- ½ cup (110 grams) firmly packed light brown sugar
- ¼ cup (57 grams) unsalted butter, melted

CAKE:
- 2 cups (250 grams) all-purpose flour
- 1 teaspoon (5 grams) baking powder
- ½ teaspoon (1.5 grams) kosher salt
- ¼ teaspoon (1.25 grams) baking soda
- ½ cup (113 grams) unsalted butter, room temperature
- 1½ cups (300 grams) granulated sugar
- 2 large eggs (100 grams), room temperature
- 2 teaspoons (8 grams) almond extract
- ½ teaspoon (2 grams) vanilla extract
- ¾ cup (180 grams) sour cream, room temperature
- 1 cup (164 grams) fresh cherries, pitted and cut in half
- ½ cup (56 grams) sliced almonds

Confectioners' sugar, for dusting

1. Preheat oven to 350°F (180°C). Using a pastry brush, brush a 9-inch springform pan with Cake Release (recipe on page 31) or spray with baking spray with flour.
2. For the topping: In a medium bowl, stir together flour, brown sugar, and melted butter until sandy and crumbs start to form. Cover and refrigerate until ready to use.
3. For the cake: In a medium bowl, whisk together flour, baking powder, salt, and baking soda.
4. In the bowl of a stand mixer fitted with the paddle attachment, beat butter on medium-low speed until smooth and creamy, about 3 minutes. Add granulated sugar, and continue to beat until fluffy, about 2 minutes, scraping down sides of bowl. Add eggs, one at a time, ensuring each egg is fully incorporated prior to adding the next. Beat in extracts.
5. With mixer on low speed, gradually add sour cream alternately with flour mixture, beginning with sour cream and ending with flour mixture, beating until just combined after each addition. Scrape down sides and bottom of bowl. Spoon batter into prepared pan, smoothing top. Top with cherries, topping, and almonds.
6. Bake until a wooden pick inserted in center comes out clean, 1 hour to 1 hour and 10 minutes. Let cool in pan on a wire rack for 10 minutes. Remove from pan, and let cool completely. Using a small, fine-mesh strainer, dust with confectioners' sugar.

# almond croissant loaf

MAKES 1 (9-INCH) LOAF

*One of my favorite mottos in life is "treat yourself!" We all work hard, and sometimes (often), we deserve a treat. Enter the Almond Croissant Loaf. A flaky, buttery croissant loaf is filled with frangipane and topped with almonds and confectioners' sugar. It's the perfect mix of comforting and indulgent for when you need a little treat.*

SYRUP:
- ½ cup (120 grams) water
- ¼ cup (50 grams) granulated sugar
- 1 teaspoon (4 grams) vanilla extract

FRANGIPANE:
- ¾ cup (170 grams) salted butter, room temperature
- 1½ cups (250 grams) granulated sugar
- 1 large egg (50 grams), room temperature
- 1½ teaspoons (6 grams) almond extract
- ½ teaspoon (2 grams) vanilla extract
- 1½ cups (144 grams) almond flour
- ⅓ cup (42 grams) all-purpose flour
- ½ teaspoon (1.5 grams) kosher salt

Croissant Loaf (recipe on page 106)
- ½ cup (57 grams) sliced almonds
- ¼ cup (30 grams) confectioners' sugar

**1.** For the syrup: In a small saucepan, bring ½ cup (120 grams) water and granulated sugar to a boil; boil for 5 minutes. Remove from heat, and let cool for 20 to 30 minutes. Add vanilla extract, stirring until combined.

**2.** Preheat oven to 350°F (180°C). Line a baking sheet with parchment paper.

**3.** For the frangipane: In a large bowl, beat butter and granulated sugar with a handheld mixer on medium speed until fluffy and combined, about 2 minutes. Add egg, and continue to beat for about 30 seconds. Add extracts, beating just until combined. Gradually add flours and salt, beating until smooth.

**4.** Cut Croissant Loaf in half horizontally. Place bottom on prepared pan. Spread three-fourths of frangipane (about 1¾ cups and 453 grams) on bottom half of loaf, smoothing to ensure bottom is completely coated. Cover with top half of loaf, and dollop remaining frangipane on top. Using a pastry brush, brush with syrup, and sprinkle with almonds.

**5.** Bake until frangipane is golden brown, about 25 minutes. Immediately dust with confectioners' sugar. Let cool completely on a wire rack.

# *double-glazed almond pound cake*

MAKES 1 (10- TO 12-CUP) BUNDT CAKE

*White chocolate ganache and raspberry glaze atop an almond-flavored pound cake is one of those desserts you'll never forget. The tender almond pound cake provides the nutty base layer while creamy white chocolate and tart raspberry add a delightful balance of flavors.*

CAKE:
- 3 cups (375 grams) all-purpose flour
- ½ teaspoon (1.5 grams) kosher salt
- ¼ teaspoon (1.25 grams) baking soda
- 1½ cups (340 grams) unsalted butter, room temperature
- 3 cups (600 grams) plus 2 tablespoons (24 grams) granulated sugar, divided
- 6 large eggs (300 grams), room temperature
- 1 tablespoon (13 grams) almond extract
- ½ cup (120 grams) sour cream, room temperature

RASPBERRY GLAZE:
- 1½ cups (188 grams) fresh raspberries
- 2 tablespoons (24 grams) granulated sugar
- 1 tablespoon (15 grams) fresh lemon juice
- 1¼ cups (150 grams) confectioners' sugar
- 2 to 3 tablespoons (30 to 45 grams) whole milk

WHITE CHOCOLATE GLAZE:
- 4 ounces (113 grams) quality white chocolate, chopped
- 4 tablespoons (60 grams) heavy whipping cream
- 1 to 2 tablespoons (8 to 16 grams) confectioners' sugar

Garnish: sliced almonds

1. Preheat oven to 325°F (170°C).
2. For the cake: In a medium bowl, whisk together flour, salt, and baking soda.
3. In the bowl of a stand mixer fitted with the paddle attachment, beat butter on medium speed until smooth, about 2 minutes. Add 3 cups (600 grams) granulated sugar, and continue to beat until fluffy, about 5 minutes, scraping down sides of bowl. Add eggs, one at a time, ensuring each egg is fully incorporated prior to adding the next, frequently scraping down sides of bowl. Beat for 1 minute. Beat in almond extract. With mixer on low speed, beat in half of flour mixture until just combined. Add sour cream, beating until just combined. Beat in remaining flour mixture just until combined, scraping down sides of bowl.
4. Using a pastry brush, brush a 10- to 12-cup Bundt pan with Cake Release (recipe on page 31) or spray with baking spray with flour. Coat pan with remaining 2 tablespoons (24 grams) sugar. Tap out any excess. Spoon batter into prepared pan, smoothing top.
5. Bake until a wooden pick inserted near center comes out clean, 1 hour and 10 minutes to 1 hour and 20 minutes. Let cool in pan on a wire rack for 5 minutes. Invert cake onto a wire rack, and unmold from pan. Let cool completely.
6. For the raspberry glaze: In a small saucepan, bring raspberries, granulated sugar, and lemon juice to a boil over medium heat; boil, stirring constantly, until sugar dissolves and sauce has thickened, 10 to 15 minutes. Remove from heat.
7. Strain mixture through a fine-mesh sieve into a medium heatproof bowl. Whisk in confectioners' sugar and milk to desired consistency. Let cool completely.
8. For the white chocolate glaze: In a medium microwave-safe bowl, microwave white chocolate and 2 tablespoons (30 grams) cream on high for 30 seconds; stir. Microwave in 15-second intervals, stirring well between each, until white chocolate is fully melted. Whisk in confectioners' sugar and remaining 2 tablespoons (30 grams) cream to desired consistency. Let cool completely, whisking before use. Pour raspberry glaze and white chocolate glaze on top of cooled cake.

# butter pecan cupcakes

MAKES 12 CUPCAKES

*Topped with a vanilla bean buttercream and toasted pecans, these tender cupcakes offer a delightful contrast in textures, making them a treat everyone will adore.*

BUTTER PECANS:
- 4 ounces (113 grams) whole pecans
- 2 tablespoons (28 grams) unsalted butter, room temperature
- 2 tablespoons (24 grams) granulated sugar
- ¼ teaspoon kosher salt

CUPCAKES:
- ½ cup plus 2 tablespoons (150 grams) whole buttermilk, room temperature
- 2 large eggs (100 grams), room temperature
- 2 tablespoons (28 grams) vegetable oil
- 1 teaspoon (4 grams) vanilla extract
- 1¾ cups (219 grams) all-purpose flour
- ¾ cup (165 grams) firmly packed light brown sugar
- ½ cup (113 grams) unsalted butter, cubed and room temperature
- ¼ cup (50 grams) granulated sugar
- 2 teaspoons (10 grams) baking powder
- ½ teaspoon (1.5 grams) kosher salt

FROSTING:
- 1 cup (227 grams) unsalted butter, room temperature
- 4 cups (480 grams) confectioners' sugar
- 6 to 8 tablespoons (90 to 120 grams) heavy whipping cream
- 1 teaspoon (6 grams) vanilla bean paste
- Pinch kosher salt

1. Preheat oven to 350°F (180°C). Line a 12-cup muffin pan with paper liners. Line a baking sheet with parchment paper.
2. For the butter pecans: In a medium bowl, stir together all ingredients until pecans are evenly coated. Spread mixture onto prepared baking sheet.
3. Bake until toasted, 12 to 15 minutes. Let cool completely. Roughly chop into smaller pieces.
4. For the cupcakes: In a medium bowl, whisk together buttermilk, eggs, oil, and vanilla extract.
5. In the bowl of a stand mixer fitted with the paddle attachment, beat flour, brown sugar, butter, granulated sugar, baking powder, and salt on medium-low speed until a sandy mixture forms. Add buttermilk mixture; continue to beat until batter is well combined and smooth, about 1 minute. Fold in half of butter pecans (about 56 grams). Divide batter among prepared muffin cups, filling each about three-fourths full.
6. Bake until a wooden pick inserted in center comes out clean, 20 to 22 minutes. Let cool completely in pans.
7. For the frosting: In the bowl of a stand mixer fitted with the paddle attachment, beat butter on medium speed for 2 minutes. Add confectioners' sugar. Gradually increase mixer speed to medium-low. Add cream and vanilla bean paste until desired consistency. Beat on medium-high speed until well combined. Add salt. Beat on high speed for 20 seconds. Transfer to a pastry bag fitted with your favorite piping tip. Pipe frosting on top of cooled cupcakes. Top with remaining butter pecans.

# matcha-and-almond sablés
## WITH WHITE CHOCOLATE DRIZZLE

MAKES ABOUT 18 COOKIES

*Afternoon tea and matcha cookies are a match made in heaven. Buttery shortbread is flavored with matcha and crushed almonds for the most wonderful texture. White chocolate adds a creamy richness that enhances the flavor of the cookie.*

- 2¼ cups (281 grams) all-purpose flour
- ½ cup (71 grams) almonds, very finely chopped
- 3 tablespoons (18 grams) matcha powder
- ½ teaspoon (1.5 grams) kosher salt
- 1 cup (227 grams) salted butter, room temperature
- ½ cup (100 grams) granulated sugar
- ½ cup (60 grams) confectioners' sugar, plus more for dusting
- 2 large egg yolks (38 grams), room temperature
- 1 teaspoon (6 grams) vanilla bean paste
- 4 ounces (113 grams) quality white chocolate, melted

Garnish: finely chopped almonds

**1.** In a medium bowl, whisk together flour, very finely chopped almonds, matcha powder, and salt until combined.

**2.** In the bowl of a stand mixer fitted with the paddle attachment, beat butter on low speed until fluffy, about 2 minutes. Add sugars, and continue to beat until sugars dissolve and mixture is pale in color, about 2 minutes, scraping down sides of bowl. Add egg yolks; continue to beat for 1 minute. Scrape down sides and bottom of bowl. Add vanilla bean paste, and continue to beat until just combined. Add flour mixture, and continue to beat until fully combined.

**3.** Turn out dough onto a lightly floured surface, and roll into a ½-inch-thick square. Wrap in plastic wrap. Place on baking sheet, and refrigerate until set, about 1½ hours.

**4.** Preheat oven to 325°F (170°C). Line 2 baking sheets with parchment paper.

**5.** Remove plastic wrap from dough. Place on parchment lined work surface. Using a 2-inch round cutter, cut dough, rerolling scraps to use all dough. Place 2 inches apart on prepared pans.

**6.** Bake until surface is set, 15 to 16 minutes. Let cool on pans for 5 minutes. Remove from pans, and let cool completely on wire racks. Dust with confectioners' sugar. Drizzle melted white chocolate onto cooled cookies, and garnish with chopped almonds, if desired.

# pistachio-and-apricot sandwich cookies

MAKES ABOUT 12 SANDWICH COOKIES

*With each bite, savor the delicate crunch of the pistachio-infused shortbread, perfectly complemented by the fruity sweetness of the apricot preserves filling. These delightful sandwich cookies are sure to satisfy your sweet tooth and leave you reaching for seconds.*

- 3 cups (375 grams) all-purpose flour
- ½ cup (71 grams) pistachios, finely chopped
- ½ teaspoon (1.5 grams) kosher salt
- 1 cup (227 grams) salted butter, room temperature
- 1 cup (200 grams) granulated sugar
- 2 large egg yolks (38 grams)
- 1½ teaspoons (6 grams) pistachio emulsion
- 1 teaspoon (6 grams) vanilla bean paste
- ½ cup (160 grams) apricot preserves

Garnish: finely chopped pistachios

1. In a large bowl, whisk together flour, crushed pistachios, and salt.
2. In the bowl of a stand mixer fitted with the paddle attachment, beat butter and sugar on low speed until light and creamy, about 3 minutes, scraping down sides of bowl. Add egg yolks, pistachio emulsion, and vanilla bean paste, and continue to beat until smooth. Scrape down sides and bottom of bowl. Add flour mixture. Gradually increase mixer speed to medium, beating until just combined. (Dough should be crumbly.)
3. Turn out dough onto a clean surface. Gently knead dough until it sticks together and is no longer crumbly. Wrap in plastic wrap. Refrigerate until completely solid, about 2 hours.
4. Line 2 rimmed baking sheets with parchment paper.
5. Divide dough in half. Roll half of dough to ⅛-inch thickness. Using a 2½x2¼-inch fluted cutter, cut dough, and place on a prepared pan. Refrigerate for 30 minutes.
6. Roll remaining dough to ⅛-inch thickness. Using a 2½x2¼-inch fluted cutter, cut dough. Using a 1½x1-inch fluted cutter, cut center from dough rectangles. Place on remaining prepared pan. Refrigerate for 30 minutes.
7. Preheat oven to 300°F (150°C).
8. Bake, one pan at a time, until edges are set and slightly golden, 8 to 10 minutes. Let cool completely on pans.
9. Spread 1 to 1½ teaspoons (7 to 10.5 grams) preserves onto flat side of whole cookies. Place cookies with cutouts, flat side down, on top of preserves. Garnish with chopped pistachios, if desired.

# pistachio sugar cookies

MAKES ABOUT 12 COOKIES

*These cookies were my father's idea. He loves pistachios, probably because he's a nut himself. (I say this lovingly, of course. Love you, Daddy!) I made my first batch, and my father ate them all. They are truly that good. It's a tender cookie with a few pistachios throughout and topped with a little pistachio glaze. Who could blame him?*

COOKIES:
- 2¼ cups (281 grams) all-purpose flour
- 1 teaspoon (5 grams) baking soda
- ½ teaspoon (1.5 grams) kosher salt
- ⅛ teaspoon ground nutmeg
- ¾ cup (170 grams) unsalted butter, room temperature
- 1¼ cups (250 grams) granulated sugar, divided
- 1 large egg (50 grams), room temperature
- 1 large egg yolk (19 grams), room temperature
- 1 teaspoon (4 grams) pistachio emulsion
- ½ teaspoon (2 grams) vanilla extract

GLAZE:
- 1 cup (120 grams) confectioners' sugar
- 2 tablespoons (30 grams) whole milk
- ½ teaspoon (2 grams) vanilla extract

Garnish: finely chopped toasted salted pistachios

**1.** Preheat oven to 350°F (180°C). Line 2 rimmed baking sheets with parchment paper.

**2.** For the cookies: In a medium bowl, whisk together flour, baking soda, salt, and nutmeg.

**3.** In the bowl of a stand mixer fitted with the paddle attachment, beat butter on medium speed until fluffy, about 2 minutes. Scrape down sides of bowl. Add 1 cup (200 grams) granulated sugar, and continue to beat until pale and fluffy, about 2 minutes. Scrape down sides of bowl. Add egg and egg yolk, and continue to beat until fully combined. Stop and scrape down sides of bowl. Add pistachio emulsion and vanilla extract, and continue to beat until well combined and smooth. With mixer on low speed, gradually add flour mixture, beating until just combined.

**4.** In a shallow bowl, place remaining ¼ cup (50 grams) granulated sugar.

**5.** Using a 3-tablespoon spring-loaded scoop, scoop dough, and roll into balls. Roll dough balls in sugar, and place about 2 inches apart on prepared pans (6 per pan).

**6.** Bake, one pan at a time, until edges are set and centers are puffy, 11 to 12 minutes. Let cool on pans for 5 minutes. Using a spatula, remove from pans, and let cool completely on a wire rack.

**7.** For the glaze: In a medium bowl, whisk together all ingredients. Let stand for 5 minutes. Drizzle glaze onto cooled cookies. Sprinkle with chopped pistachios, if desired.

# milk chocolate-and-hazelnut scones

**MAKES ABOUT 9 SCONES**

*Hazelnut and chocolate are already best friends, so what better way to celebrate this friendship than by putting hazelnuts into a scone and topping it with milk chocolate? The smoothness of the milk chocolate with the crunchy hazelnuts makes me feel like I'm eating a candy bar scone. I just adore this recipe, especially with a cup of tea.*

| | |
|---|---|
| 2½ | cups (313 grams) all-purpose flour, plus more for dusting |
| 1 | cup (96 grams) hazelnut flour |
| ½ | cup (100 grams) granulated sugar |
| 1 | tablespoon (15 grams) baking powder |
| 2 | teaspoons (6 grams) kosher salt |
| ¼ | teaspoon ground nutmeg |
| 1 | cup (227 grams) cold salted butter, cubed |
| ⅔ | cup (160 grams) sour cream, room temperature |
| 1 | large egg (50 grams), room temperature |
| 1 | teaspoon (4 grams) vanilla extract |
| 3 | tablespoons (45 grams) heavy whipping cream |
| 3.5 | ounces (100 grams) quality milk chocolate, chopped |

Garnish: chopped hazelnuts

**1.** Preheat oven to 400°F (200°C). Line a baking sheet with parchment paper.

**2.** In a medium bowl, whisk together all-purpose flour, hazelnut flour, sugar, baking powder, salt, and nutmeg. Add cold butter. Using your hands, cut butter into flour mixture until mixture is crumbly and largest butter pieces are pea-size.

**3.** In a small bowl, whisk together sour cream, egg, and vanilla extract. Add sour cream mixture to flour mixture, and stir until a shaggy dough forms. (Dough may be very crumbly, but do not add more sour cream.)

**4.** Lightly dust work surface with all-purpose flour. Turn out dough onto surface, and gently knead dough until it is no longer crumbly. Pat into a 1-inch-thick rectangle. Using a sharp kitchen knife, cut into quarters. Stack quarters on top of each other, and pat down into a ¾-inch-thick rectangle. Repeat cutting, stacking, and patting 2 more times. Pat dough to ¾-inch-thick rectangle. Using a sharp kitchen knife, cut into 8 even triangles. Fold together any excess dough, and repeat until all dough is used. Place on prepared pan, and freeze for 15 minutes.

**5.** Using a pastry brush, brush dough with cream.

**6.** Bake until golden brown and flaky layers are visible, 20 to 25 minutes. Let cool on pan for 5 minutes. Remove from pan, and let cool completely on a wire rack.

**7.** Meanwhile, in a microwave-safe small bowl, microwave chocolate on high in 10-second intervals, stirring between each, until melted. Drizzle a generous amount of melted chocolate on top of scones. Sprinkle with chopped hazelnuts, if desired.

# sticky bun babka

**MAKES 1 (8½X4½-INCH) LOAF**

*Indulge in the delight of babka, where each soft layer is swirled with cinnamon and studded with toasted pecans, all enveloped in a rich caramel glaze that oozes with sweetness.*

**BREAD:**
- ½ cup (120 grams) warm whole milk (105°F/41°C to 110°F/43°C)
- 4 tablespoons (48 grams) granulated sugar
- 1½ teaspoons (4.5 grams) active dry yeast
- 2½ cups (283 grams) bread flour, plus more for dusting
- 1 large egg (50 grams)
- 1½ teaspoons (4.5 grams) kosher salt
- 5 tablespoons (70 grams) unsalted butter, room temperature

**FILLING:**
- 1 cup (142 grams) pecans, chopped
- ½ cup (110 grams) firmly packed light brown sugar
- 5 tablespoons (70 grams) unsalted butter, room temperature
- 2 teaspoons (4 grams) ground cinnamon
- ¼ teaspoon kosher salt

**EGG WASH:**
- 1 large egg (50 grams)
- 1 tablespoon (15 grams) water

**STICKY SAUCE:**
- ½ cup (110 grams) firmly packed light brown sugar
- ¼ cup (57 grams) unsalted butter
- 3 tablespoons (63 grams) honey
- 1 tablespoon (15 grams) heavy whipping cream
- ½ teaspoon (1 gram) ground cinnamon
- Pinch kosher salt

**1.** For the bread: In the bowl of a stand mixer, stir together warm milk, 1 tablespoon (12 grams) sugar, and yeast by hand. Let stand until bloomed and foaming, 5 to 10 minutes. Add flour, egg, salt, and remaining 3 tablespoons (36 grams) granulated sugar.

**2.** Fit stand mixer with the dough hook attachment. Knead on low speed and then gradually increase mixer speed to medium, kneading until a cohesive dough forms and pulls away from sides of bowl, 3 to 4 minutes. Add butter, 1 tablespoon (14 grams) at a time, kneading until combined after each addition. Continue to knead for 6 to 8 minutes. Do the windowpane test. (See Pro Tip on page 35.)

**3.** Place dough in a well-oiled bowl. Cover and let rise in a warm, draft-free place (75°F/24°C) until doubled in size, 1 to 1½ hours.

**4.** For the filling: In a small bowl, stir together all ingredients until a thick paste forms, 1 to 2 minutes.

**5.** Spray and line an 8½x4½-inch loaf pan with parchment paper, letting excess extend over sides of pan.

**6.** Punch down dough, and turn out on a lightly floured surface. Using a rolling pin, roll dough into a 14x10-inch rectangle. Spread filling all over dough. Starting with one long side, tightly roll up dough into a log, and pinch seam to seal. Using a serrated knife, cut off any excess dough on ends of log. Cut log in half lengthwise, leaving one end of log intact. Twist pieces of log, cut side up, around each other, and pinch ends to seal. Place in prepared pan. Cover and let rise in a warm, draft-free place (75°C/24°C) until puffy, 45 minutes to 1 hour.

**7.** Preheat oven to 350°F (180°C).

**8.** For the egg wash: In a small bowl, whisk together egg and 1 tablespoon (15 grams) water. Using a pastry brush, brush tops of rolls with egg wash.

**9.** Bake until golden brown and a wooden pick inserted into center comes out with a few crumbs, 40 to 50 minutes. Let cool in pan for 5 minutes. Remove from pan, and place on a wire rack over a rimmed baking sheet.

**10.** Meanwhile, for the sticky sauce: In a small saucepan, combine brown sugar, butter, and honey. Cook over medium-low heat, stirring constantly, until butter is melted and mixture is smooth and syrupy, 3 to 5 minutes. Remove from heat. Stir in cream, cinnamon, and salt. Pour sauce on top of hot bread.

# from the garden

# lavender cupcakes
## WITH LIME SWISS MERINGUE BUTTERCREAM

MAKES 12 CUPCAKES

*These cupcakes are full of fragrant lavender, giving them a floral aroma that's both calming and refreshing. A zesty lime Swiss meringue buttercream adds a bright and tangy contrast, creating a harmonious balance of flavors that dance on the palate.*

CUPCAKES:
- ½ cup plus 2 tablespoons (150 grams) whole buttermilk, room temperature
- 2 large eggs (100 grams), room temperature
- 2 tablespoons (28 grams) vegetable oil
- 1½ teaspoons (9 grams) vanilla bean paste
- 1¾ cups (219 grams) cake flour
- 1 cup (200 grams) granulated sugar
- ½ cup (113 grams) salted butter, room temperature
- 1 tablespoon (2 grams) dried culinary lavender
- 2 teaspoons (10 grams) baking powder
- ½ teaspoon (1.5 grams) kosher salt

BUTTERCREAM (SEE NOTE):
- 5 cups Swiss Meringue Buttercream (see page 27)
- 3 tablespoons (6 grams) lime zest
- ¼ cup (60 grams) fresh lime juice

Garnish: lime wedges, dried culinary lavender

**1.** Preheat oven to 350°F (180°C). Line a 12-cup muffin pan with paper liners.

**2.** For the cupcakes: In a medium bowl, whisk together buttermilk, eggs, oil, and vanilla bean paste until well combined.

**3.** In the bowl of a stand mixer fitted with the paddle attachment, beat flour, granulated sugar, butter, lavender, baking powder, and salt on medium-low speed until mixture has sandy texture and butter is fully incorporated, 1 to 2 minutes. Add buttermilk mixture, and continue to beat until batter is well combined and smooth, 1 to 2 minutes. Scrape down sides and bottom of bowl. Continue to beat until batter is well combined and smooth, 10 to 15 seconds. Divide batter evenly among prepared muffin cups, filling each about two-thirds full.

**4.** Bake until a wooden pick inserted in center comes out with a few moist crumbs, 20 to 25 minutes. Let cool completely in pan.

**5.** For the buttercream: In the bowl of a stand mixer fitted with the whisk attachment, add Swiss Meringue Buttercream, lime zest, and lime juice, 1 tablespoon (15 grams) at a time, beating at medium speed until combined after each addition. Switch to the paddle attachment. Beat on the lowest speed until all air bubbles are removed, 1 to 2 minutes. Transfer to a 12-inch pastry bag fitted with your favorite piping tip. Pipe buttercream on top of cooled cupcakes. Garnish with lime wedges and lavender, if desired.

**NOTE:** *This recipe makes a lot of buttercream, so if you don't like a lot of frosting on your cupcakes, cut the frosting recipe in half.*

# lemon-and-fennel shortbread cookies

**MAKES ABOUT 33 COOKIES**

*Blending the bright zest of lemon with the subtle licorice notes of fennel, these cookies are wonderfully crisp and buttery, offering a refreshing twist on classic shortbread.*

COOKIES:
- 3 cups (375 grams) all-purpose flour, plus more for dusting
- 2 tablespoons (18 grams) fennel seeds
- 1 teaspoon (3 grams) kosher salt
- 1¼ cups (250 grams) granulated sugar
- 2 tablespoons (6 grams) lemon zest
- 1 cup (227 grams) salted butter, room temperature
- 1 large egg (50 grams)
- 1 large egg yolk (19 grams)
- 2 teaspoons (8 grams) lemon extract
- 1 teaspoon (6 grams) vanilla bean paste

GLAZE:
- 2 cups (240 grams) confectioners' sugar
- 3 to 4 tablespoons (45 to 60 grams) fresh lemon juice

Garnish: lemon zest, fennel seeds

**1.** Line baking sheets with parchment paper.
**2.** For the cookies: In a medium bowl, whisk together flour, fennel seeds, and salt.
**3.** In a small bowl, pinch together granulated sugar and lemon zest until fragrant and sugar takes on a pale yellow color. (The color changes as the oils from the lemon zest are expressed on the sugar, enhancing that lemon flavor!)
**4.** In the bowl of a stand mixer fitted with the paddle attachment, beat butter and lemon sugar on medium speed until light and fluffy, about 3 minutes, scraping down sides of bowl. Add egg and egg yolk; continue to beat until combined. Scrape down sides of bowl. Add lemon extract and vanilla bean paste; continue to beat until combined, about 30 seconds. Add flour mixture, and beat on low speed until combined.
**5.** Turn out dough onto a lightly floured surface. Roll into a ½-inch-thick rectangle. Using a 2-inch round cutter, cut dough, rerolling scraps to use all dough. Place on prepared pans, and refrigerate for 1 hour.
**6.** Preheat oven to 300°F (150°C). Line rimmed baking sheets with parchment paper.
**7.** Place dough rounds 2 inches apart on prepared pans.
**8.** Bake, one pan at a time, until edges are just barely golden, 25 to 30 minutes. Let cool on pans for 2 minutes. Remove from pans, and let cool completely on wire racks.
**9.** For the glaze: In a medium bowl, whisk together confectioners' sugar and lemon juice until desired consistency is reached. Dunk tops of cooled cookies into glaze. Place, glaze side up, on wire racks. Garnish with lemon zest and fennel seeds, if desired. Let stand until glaze is set.

# lavender meringue cookies

MAKES ABOUT 124 COOKIES

*These Lavender Meringue Cookies are delicate, ethereal treats that enchant you with their subtle floral notes and crisp, airy texture. Each bite dissolves blissfully on the tongue, releasing a whisper of lavender that's both calming and luxurious.*

- 1 tablespoon (5 grams) fresh lemon juice
- 3 large egg whites (120 grams), room temperature
- ½ cup (100 grams) granulated sugar
- ¼ teaspoon cream of tartar
- 1 teaspoon (6 grams) vanilla bean paste
- ½ teaspoon (3 grams) lavender paste
- Pinch kosher salt

1. Preheat oven to 200°F (93°C). Place silicone baking mats on 3 rimmed baking sheets.
2. In the bowl of a stand mixer, place lemon juice. Using a paper towel, wipe down sides and bottom of bowl with lemon juice until nothing remains. (This will help remove any oils and excess moisture from the bowl.) Let dry.
3. In the top of a double boiler, whisk together egg whites and sugar. Cook over simmering water, whisking frequently, until sugar fully dissolves and an instant-read thermometer registers 150°F (65°C). (Sugar is dissolved when you can rub the mixture between your fingers and feel no sugar.)
4. Transfer egg white mixture to the cleaned bowl of a stand mixer fitted with the whisk attachment. Beat on low speed until bubbly, about 2 minutes. Add cream of tartar, and beat on medium speed until stiff peaks form and meringue is glossy and white, 7 to 10 minutes. Add vanilla bean paste, lavender paste, and salt. Whisk until just combined. Transfer to a 12-inch pastry bag fitted with a ½-inch open star piping tip. Pipe meringue into 1-inch kisses on prepared pan. (Pipe all meringue at this time. You cannot store meringue to make later. It will become syrupy.)
5. Bake until meringues look dry and easily lift off pan, 1 hour to 1 hour and 20 minutes. (If meringues feel mushy when you touch them, continue to bake for 5 to 10 minutes more. Watch closely; if they turn golden brown, they're overbaked.) Turn off oven, and prop oven door open so it's ajar. Let meringues cool in oven for 2 hours.

## WITH CHAMPAGNE FROSTING

MAKES 12 CUPCAKES

*Romantic and floral, this recipe reminds me of Valentine's Day. The cupcakes, flavored with rose water, serve as our soft, floral base. Then they are crowned with a Champagne frosting that's both silky and effervescent, adding a sophisticated touch to the delicate flavors.*

CUPCAKES:
- ½ cup plus 2 tablespoons (150 grams) whole milk
- 2 large eggs (100 grams)
- 2 tablespoons (28 grams) vegetable oil
- 1 teaspoon (4 grams) rose water
- 1 teaspoon (6 grams) vanilla bean paste
- 1½ cups (188 grams) all-purpose flour
- 1 cup (200 grams) granulated sugar
- ½ cup (113 grams) unsalted butter, room temperature, cubed
- 2 teaspoons (10 grams) baking powder
- ½ teaspoon (1.5 grams) kosher salt

FROSTING:
- 1 cup (227 grams) unsalted butter, room temperature
- 5 cups (600 grams) confectioners' sugar
- ¼ teaspoon (1 gram) lemon extract
- Pinch kosher salt
- 3 tablespoons (45 grams) Champagne

Garnish: chopped dried rose petals

**1.** Preheat oven to 350°F (180°C). Line a 12-cup muffin pan with paper liners.

**2.** For the cupcakes: In a medium bowl, whisk together milk, eggs, oil, rose water, and vanilla bean paste.

**3.** In the bowl of a stand mixer fitted with the paddle attachment, beat flour, granulated sugar, butter, baking powder, and salt on medium speed until a sandy mixture forms and butter is fully incorporated, 1 to 2 minutes. Add milk mixture, and continue to beat until smooth, about 30 seconds. Scrape down sides of bowl. Continue to beat until smooth, 10 to 15 seconds. Divide batter among prepared muffin cups, filling each about two-thirds full.

**4.** Bake until a wooden pick inserted in center comes out clean, 20 to 22 minutes. Let cool in pan for 5 to 10 minutes. Remove from pan, and let cool completely on a wire rack.

**5.** For the frosting: In the bowl of a stand mixer fitted with the paddle attachment, beat butter on medium speed until creamy, about 1 minute. Add confectioners' sugar, lemon extract, and salt. Gradually increase mixer speed to medium, and beat until smooth, 1 to 2 minutes. Add Champagne, 1 tablespoon (15 grams) at a time, beating until there are no streaks left after each addition, about 15 seconds each. Transfer to a 12-inch pastry bag fitted with your favorite piping tip. Pipe frosting onto cooled cupcakes. Garnish with rose petals, if desired.

# sage browned butter doughnuts

MAKES ABOUT 10 DOUGHNUTS

*Soft cake doughnuts are fried to a golden crisp and then glazed with a sage-infused browned butter topping that melts into every crumb. The combination of aromatic sage and caramellike browned butter creates a savory-sweet taste that's welcome any time of day.*

DOUGHNUTS:
- 3 cups (375 grams) cake flour, plus more for dusting
- 2 teaspoons (10 grams) baking powder
- 1 teaspoon (3 grams) kosher salt
- ¼ teaspoon ground nutmeg
- ¾ cup (150 grams) granulated sugar
- 12 fresh sage leaves (3 grams), diced
- 3 tablespoons (42 grams) salted butter, room temperature
- 2 large egg yolks (38 grams), room temperature
- 1 teaspoon (4 grams) vanilla extract
- 1 cup (240 grams) sour cream, room temperature
- Vegetable oil, for frying

GLAZE:
- ¼ cup (57 grams) salted butter
- 6 fresh sage leaves (1.5 grams)
- 1 cup (120 grams) confectioners' sugar
- 3 tablespoons (45 grams) heavy whipping cream
- 1 teaspoon (4 grams) vanilla extract
- Pinch kosher salt

**1.** For the doughnuts: In a medium bowl, sift together flour, baking powder, salt, and nutmeg.
**2.** In a small bowl, add granulated sugar and sage. Using your fingers, pinch together until fragrant.
**3.** In a large bowl, beat butter with a handheld mixer on medium speed until light and creamy, about 2 minutes. Add sage sugar, and continue to beat until fluffy, about 3 minutes. Add egg yolks and vanilla extract, and continue to beat until combined, about 2 minutes. Gradually add flour mixture alternately with sour cream, beginning and ending with flour mixture, folding with a silicone spatula until just combined after each addition. Cover and refrigerate until firm, about 2 hours, or up to overnight.
**4.** Turn out dough onto a well-floured surface, and roll to ½-inch thickness. Using a 3-inch round cutter, cut dough. Using a ½-inch round cutter (or the top of a soda bottle), cut out center of each dough round. Reroll scraps to use all dough. Place on a parchment lined baking sheet, and refrigerate for 20 minutes.
**5.** In a large heavy-bottomed pot, pour oil to a depth of 2 inches, and heat over medium heat until a deep-fry thermometer registers 350°F (180°C).
**6.** Fry doughnuts in batches until golden brown, 2 to 3 minutes per side. Using a spider strainer or slotted spoon, remove doughnuts from oil, and let drain on a wire rack. Let cool for 20 minutes.
**7.** For the glaze: In a medium skillet, melt butter over medium heat. Add sage, and cook, stirring constantly, until fragrant and crispy, 2 to 4 minutes. Remove sage leaves, and let drain on a paper towel. Set aside.
**8.** Continue to cook butter until butter is a medium-brown color and has a nutty aroma. Transfer to a medium bowl. Add confectioners' sugar, cream, vanilla extract, and salt. Whisk until smooth and mixture begins to thicken, 2 to 3 minutes. Dip tops of doughnuts into glaze. Place, glaze side up, on a wire rack, and let stand until glaze is set. Garnish with fried sage leaves, if desired.

"baking is about transformation.
turning flour into cakes,
eggs into custard, and
ideas into something real."

— BARBARA KAFKA

# lemon-basil trifles

MAKES 6 SERVINGS

*Lemon-Basil Trifles blend the zesty brightness of lemon curd with the aromatic promise of basil, all layered beautifully with luscious butter cake. Each spoonful is a dreamy escape into a flavor combination that dances between sweet, citrusy, and herby.*

CAKE:
- 1¾ cups (219 grams) all-purpose flour
- 1½ teaspoons (7.5 grams) baking powder
- ½ teaspoon (1.5 grams) kosher salt
- ⅛ teaspoon ground nutmeg
- 1 cup (227 grams) salted butter, room temperature
- 1 cup (200 grams) granulated sugar
- 3 large eggs (150 grams), room temperature
- 2 tablespoons (30 grams) heavy whipping cream, room temperature
- 2 teaspoons (8 grams) vanilla extract

LEMON CURD:
- 5 large egg yolks (95 grams)
- 1 cup (200 grams) granulated sugar
- 2 tablespoons (12 grams) lemon zest
- ⅓ cup (80 grams) fresh lemon juice
- 5 tablespoons (70 grams) unsalted butter
- ½ teaspoon (2 grams) lemon extract

WHIPPED CREAM:
- 1¼ cups (300 grams) heavy whipping cream
- ½ cup (60 grams) confectioners' sugar
- 5 fresh basil leaves (5 grams), finely chopped

Garnish: fresh basil leaves, halved fresh strawberries

1. Preheat oven to 350°F (180°C). Spray an 8½x4½-inch loaf pan with cooking spray. Line pan with parchment paper.
2. For the cake: In a medium bowl, whisk together flour, baking powder, salt, and nutmeg.
3. In the bowl of a stand mixer fitted with the paddle attachment, beat butter and granulated sugar on medium speed until fluffy, about 3 minutes, scraping down sides of bowl. Add eggs, one at a time, ensuring each egg is fully incorporated prior to adding the next, 20 to 40 seconds each. Add cream and vanilla extract, and continue to beat until fully incorporated, about 1 minute. Fold in flour mixture with a large spoon or silicone spatula until fully incorporated, about 1 minute. Spread batter into prepared pan.
4. Bake until a wooden pick inserted in center comes out clean, 1 hour to 1 hour and 10 minutes. Let cool in pan for 10 minutes. Remove from pan, and let cool completely on a wire rack. Slice cake into small bite-size chunks (about the size of rolling dice or ice cubes).
5. For the lemon curd: In a heatproof bowl, combine egg yolks, granulated sugar, and lemon zest and juice. Place bowl over a saucepan of simmering water. Cook, whisking every 30 seconds, until mixture begins to thicken, 10 to 15 minutes. Remove from heat, and add butter and lemon extract, whisking until butter is fully melted and combined, 2 to 3 minutes. Let cool completely. , or refrigerate until ready to use.
6. For whipped cream: In a large bowl, beat cold cream, confectioners' sugar, and finely chopped basil with a handheld mixer on medium speed until medium-stiff peaks form, 3 to 4 minutes.
7. To assemble: Spoon a generous amount of lemon curd into bottom of individual serving cups. Layer with cake pieces, and top with whipped cream. Repeat layers to completely fill each cup. Garnish with basil leaves and strawberries, if desired.

# orange blossom crème brûlées

**MAKES 6 CRÈME BRÛLÉES**

*Pairing the traditional richness of crème brûlée with a refreshing floral flavor, this sophisticated treat transports your sense to a blossoming orange grove with every bite.*

CRÈME BRÛLÉES:
- 2 cups (480 grams) heavy whipping cream
- 5 large egg yolks (95 grams)
- ½ cup (100 grams) plus 6 teaspoons (24 grams) granulated sugar, divided
- 2 teaspoons (8 grams) orange blossom water
- ½ teaspoon (2 grams) vanilla extract
- Pinch kosher salt

Boiling water

WHIPPED CREAM:
- ½ cup (120 grams) cold heavy whipping cream
- 3 tablespoons (60 grams) apricot preserves

Garnish: orange blossoms

**1.** Preheat oven to 300°F (150°C).

**2.** For the crème brûlées: In a small saucepan, bring cream to a simmer over medium-low heat.

**3.** In a large bowl, whisk together egg yolks, ½ cup (100 grams) sugar, and orange blossom water until pale yellow and fluffy, 2 to 3 minutes. Add warm cream, ½ cup (120 grams) at a time, whisking constantly to ensure eggs do not cook. Add vanilla and salt, whisking until combined, about 30 seconds.

**4.** Place 6 (6-ounce) ramekins in a baking pan. Spoon ½ cup egg yolk mixture into each ramekin. Place pan in oven. Pour boiling water into baking pan until water covers bottom one-fourth of ramekins.

**5.** Bake until edges are set but centers are still jiggly, 30 to 45 minutes. Carefully transfer ramekins to a wire rack, and let cool for 1 hour. Refrigerate for at least 2 hours.

**6.** Just before serving, sprinkle remaining 6 teaspoons (24 grams) sugar onto crème brûlées (1 teaspoon or 4 grams each). Using a handheld kitchen torch, carefully brown sugar.

**7.** For the whipped cream: In a large bowl, beat cold cream and preserves with a handheld mixer on medium speed until stiff peaks form. Dollop cream on top of crème brûlées. Garnish with orange blossoms, if desired.

# strawberry-lavender eton mess

MAKES 4 TO 5 SERVINGS

*A whimsical twist on a classic British dessert, layers of crumbled lavender-infused meringues, lush strawberry sauce, and rich whipped cream create a fragrant, delicate treat.*

- 2 pounds (907 grams) fresh strawberries, hulled and halved
- 1 cup (200 grams) granulated sugar
- 1 tablespoon (15 grams) fresh lemon juice
- 1 tablespoon (8 grams) cornstarch
- 1 tablespoon (15 grams) water
- Pinch kosher salt
- 2 cups (480 grams) cold heavy whipping cream
- ¾ cup (90 grams) confectioners' sugar
- 1 teaspoon (6 grams) vanilla bean paste
- Lavender Meringue Cookies (recipe on page 145)
- Garnish: Lavender Meringue Cookies, fresh mint leaves

**1.** In a medium saucepan, combine three-fourths of the strawberries, granulated sugar, and lemon juice. Bring to a boil over medium-low heat, and cook until strawberry juices are rendered, 5 to 7 minutes. Reduce heat to low, and simmer until strawberries are softened, about 10 minutes.

**2.** In a small bowl, whisk together cornstarch and 1 tablespoon (15 grams) water. Add cornstarch slurry to strawberry mixture in pan. Cook over medium-low heat, stirring constantly, until sauce begins to thicken, 2 to 4 minutes. Remove from heat, and stir in salt. Let cool completely.

**3.** In a large bowl, beat cold cream and confectioners' sugar with a handheld mixer on medium speed until stiff peaks form, 4 to 5 minutes. Add vanilla bean paste, beating until just combined. Carefully fold in about half of strawberry mixture, being careful not to deflate cream mixture.

**4.** In a medium bowl, crush about three-fourths of Lavender Meringue Cookies.

**5.** In individual serving bowls, evenly layer strawberry sauce, strawberry whipped cream, crushed meringues, and remaining strawberries. Garnish with remaining Lavender Meringue Cookies, mint, and lavender, if desired.

# rose sugar churros

MAKES ABOUT 22 CHURROS

*Dusted generously with a fragrant rose sugar, these churros reveal a tender, floral center that contrasts beautifully with the crispy, golden exterior.*

COATING:
- 1 cup (200 grams) granulated sugar
- 1 tablespoon (2 grams) finely chopped dried rose petals

CHURROS:
- Vegetable oil, for frying
- ¾ cup (180 grams) water
- ½ cup (113 grams) unsalted butter
- ¼ cup (60 grams) whole milk
- 2 tablespoons (24 grams) granulated sugar
- 1¼ cups (156 grams) all-purpose flour, sifted
- 1¼ teaspoons (3.75 grams) kosher salt
- 3 large eggs (150 grams), room temperature
- 2 teaspoons (10 grams) rose water

1. For coating: In a small bowl, stir together sugar and rose petals.
2. For churros: In a large heavy-bottomed saucepan, pour oil to a depth of 2 inches, and heat over medium heat until a deep-fry thermometer registers 340°F (170°C) to 350°F (180°C).
3. While the oil is heating, in a medium saucepan, bring ¾ cup (180 grams) water, butter, milk, and sugar to a boil over medium heat. Add flour and salt. Using a wooden spoon, stir until a dough begins to form. Continue to stir until a film forms on bottom of pan, about 5 minutes.
4. Transfer dough to the bowl of a stand mixer fitted with the paddle attachment. Beat on low speed until dough has cooled but is still warm to the touch, about 4 minutes. Add eggs, one at a time, ensuring each egg is fully incorporated prior to adding the next, about 15 seconds each. Add rose water, and continue to beat until just combined, 15 to 30 seconds. Transfer to a pastry bag fitted with your favoritea ½-inch open star piping tip.
5. Working in batches, carefully pipe dough in a straight line about 6 inches in length into hot oil, cutting dough with kitchen shears at end closest to piping tip when desired length is reached. Fry until golden brown, 1 to 2 minutes per side. Remove from oil, and let drain on a wire rack. Toss in rose sugar to coat.

# family favorites

# aunt hazel's citrus pound cake

**MAKES 1 (15-CUP) BUNDT CAKE**

*My aunt Hazel made THE BEST pound cakes. Whenever I'd visit her house, she'd always have a pound cake baked, and as soon as I walked in, my eyes immediately darted straight to it. She'd always give me a slice to take home, but I had no self-control and ate it in the car on the way home. She gave me her recipe one day on a piece of loose-leaf paper, but I'm convinced there was a secret ingredient in her cake because my versions never tasted exactly like hers. I've experimented and finally got it close. Even though she never called hers a citrus cake, she added orange and lemon extracts, which give it its unique flavor. I also used shortening for a more tender crumb and added in a full heaping cup of sour cream for a little tang to complement the citrusy flavors. Sadly, Aunt Hazel is no longer with us, but her pound cake will forever live in my heart! I hope this recipe does her justice.*

- 3 cups (600 grams) plus 2 tablespoons (24 grams) granulated sugar, divided
- 3 cups (375 grams) cake flour
- 1 teaspoon (3 grams) kosher salt
- ¼ teaspoon (1.25 grams) baking soda
- 1 cup (227 grams) unsalted butter, room temperature
- ½ cup (113 grams) butter-flavored shortening
- 6 large eggs (300 grams), room temperature
- 2 teaspoons (8 grams) vanilla extract
- 2 teaspoons (8 grams) lemon extract
- 1 teaspoon (4 grams) orange extract
- 1 cup (240 grams) sour cream, room temperature
- 2 to 3 tablespoons (14 to 21 grams) confectioners' sugar

**1.** Preheat oven to 325°F (170°C). Using a pastry brush, brush a 15-cup Bundt pan with Cake Release or spray with baking spray with flour. Sprinkle 2 tablespoons (24 grams) granulated sugar in pan, swirling to coat. Tap out any excess.

**2.** In a large bowl, whisk together flour, salt, and baking soda.

**3.** In the bowl of a stand mixer fitted with the paddle attachment, beat butter and shortening on medium-low speed for 1 minute. Add remaining 3 cups (600 grams) sugar, and continue to beat until light and fluffy, about 4 minutes. Scrape down sides and bottom of bowl. Add eggs, one at a time, ensuring each egg is fully incorporated prior to adding the next, scraping down sides and bottom of bowl after fourth egg and after sixth egg. With mixer on medium-low speed, add extracts. With mixer on medium-low speed, gradually add flour mixture alternately with sour cream, beginning and ending with flour mixture, beating until just combined after each addition. Spoon into prepared pan.

**4.** Bake until golden brown and a wooden pick inserted near center comes out clean, 1 hour and 10 minutes to 1 hour and 20 minutes. Let cool in pan for 10 minutes. Invert cake onto a wire rack, and unmold from pan. Let cool completely. Dust with confectioners' sugar before serving.

# cranberry bars
## WITH ORANGE SHORTBREAD CRUST

**MAKES 18 BARS**

*These bars are the perfect choice for those seeking a memorable dessert! The buttery, citrusy shortbread crust is topped with a bold layer of cranberry compote. To finish, a billowy meringue complements the rich flavor of the bars with a touch of sweetness.*

CRUST:
- 1¾ cups (219 grams) all-purpose flour
- ¾ cup (150 grams) granulated sugar
- 1 tablespoon (6 grams) orange zest
- ¼ teaspoon kosher salt
- ½ cup (113 grams) unsalted butter, cubed and room temperature

CRANBERRY CURD:
- 2 pounds (910 grams) fresh cranberries
- 2 cups (400 grams) granulated sugar
- 5 large egg yolks (95 grams), room temperature
- 2 tablespoons (16 grams) cornstarch
- 2 tablespoons (30 grams) water
- ½ teaspoon (1 gram) ground cinnamon
- 3 tablespoons (42 grams) unsalted butter

MERINGUE:
- 1 tablespoon (15 grams) fresh lemon juice
- 2 large egg whites (60 grams), room temperature
- 3 tablespoons (24 grams) granulated sugar
- ¼ teaspoon cream of tartar

**1.** Preheat oven to 350°F (180°C). Line a 9-inch square baking pan with parchment paper, letting excess extend over sides of pan.

**2.** For the crust: In a large bowl, stir together flour, sugar, orange zest, and salt. Using your hands, cut butter into flour mixture until mixture is crumbly. Press into bottom of prepared pan.

**3.** Bake until golden and puffy, 15 to 18 minutes. Let cool completely.

**4.** For the cranberry curd: In a medium saucepan, combine cranberries and sugar. Cook over medium heat, stirring frequently, until mixture comes to a boil and cranberries begins to burst, 10 to 15 minutes.

**5.** In the work bowl of a food processor, process egg yolks until combined. With food processor running, carefully pour hot cranberry mixture through food chute, processing until smooth. Return mixture to saucepan.

**6.** In a small bowl, stir together cornstarch and 2 tablespoons (30 grams) water. Pour cornstarch slurry and cinnamon into cranberry mixture, and stir until well combined. Cook over medium heat, stirring constantly, until mixture thickens and cornstarch flavor is cooked out, about 5 minutes. Stir in butter, and remove from heat. Pour cranberry mixture on top of prepared crust, and smooth with an offset spatula. Cover with plastic wrap, pressing wrap directly onto surface of curd to prevent a film from forming. Let cool at room temperature for 1 hour; refrigerate until fully set, at least 4 hours. Slice into 18 (3x1½-inch) rectangles.

**7.** For the meringue: In the bowl of a stand mixer, place lemon juice. Using a paper towel, wipe down sides and bottom of bowl with lemon juice until nothing remains. (This will help remove any oils and excess moisture from the bowl.) Let dry.

**8.** In the top of a double boiler, whisk together egg whites and sugar. Cook over simmering water, stirring occassionally, until sugar fully dissolves and an instant-read thermometer registers 150°F (66°C), 5 to 7 minutes. (Sugar is dissolved when you can rub the mixture between your fingers and feel no sugar.)

**9.** In the cleaned bowl of a stand mixer fitted with the whisk attachment, carefully place egg mixture. Beat on low speed until bubbly. Add cream of tartar, and beat on medium speed until glossy, stiff peaks form, 5 to 7 minutes. Spoon meringue into a pastry bag fitted with your favorite piping tip, and pipe on top of cranberry bars. Using kitchen torch, carefully brown meringue.

# bobbie's fave sugar cookies

**MAKES ABOUT 15 COOKIES**

*When I visit, my family always expect me to bring these. Despite all the elaborate desserts I make, these simple cookies are my family's favorite. Sometimes, you can't beat a classic!*

| | |
|---|---|
| 2½ | cups (313 grams) all-purpose flour |
| 1 | teaspoon (3 grams) kosher salt |
| ½ | teaspoon (2.5 grams) baking powder |
| ¼ | teaspoon (1.25 grams) baking soda |
| 1 | cup (227 grams) unsalted butter, softened |
| 1½ | cups (300 grams) granulated sugar, divided |
| ¼ | cup plus 1 tablespoon (69 grams) firmly packed light brown sugar |
| 1 | large egg (50 grams), room temperature |
| 1 | large egg yolk (19 grams), room temperature |
| 1 | tablespoon (18 grams) vanilla bean paste |

**1.** Preheat oven to 350°F (180°C). Line 3 baking sheets with parchment paper.

**2.** In a large bowl, whisk together flour, salt, baking powder, and baking soda.

**3.** In the bowl of a stand mixer fitted with the paddle attachment, beat butter, 1 cup (200 grams) granulated sugar, and brown sugar on medium speed until light and fluffy, about 3 minutes, scraping down sides of bowl. Add egg and egg yolk, and continue to beat until combined; scrape down sides of bowl. Add vanilla bean paste, and continue to beat for 1 minute. Add flour mixture, and beat at low speed until just combined.

**4.** In a shallow bowl, place remaining ½ cup (100 grams) granulated sugar.

**5.** Using a 3-tablespoon spring-loaded scoop, scoop dough, and roll into balls. Roll dough balls in sugar, and place about 4½ inches apart on prepared pans (4 to 5 per pan).

**6.** Bake, one pan at a time, until edges are set and centers are puffy, 13 to 15 minutes. Let cool on pans for 10 minutes. Using a spatula, remove from pans, and let cool completely on a wire rack.

# ardyn's cotton candy cupcakes

MAKES 12 CUPCAKES

*My baby girl is too young to indulge in my baked goods, but when I think of her, I think of something sweet like cotton candy. The cupcakes are flavored with cotton candy extract, and the Swiss meringue buttercream balances the sweetness by giving the cupcakes a buttery-smooth finish. These are inspired by her jovial spirit. She's always smiling, always happy, and always just so sweet.*

CUPCAKES:
- ½ cup plus 2 tablespoons (150 grams) whole buttermilk, room temperature
- 2 large eggs (100 grams), room temperature
- 2 tablespoons (28 grams) vegetable oil
- 2 teaspoons (8 grams) cotton candy flavoring
- 1 teaspoon (6 grams) vanilla bean paste
- 1¾ cups (219 grams) all-purpose flour
- 1 cup (200 grams) granulated sugar
- ½ cup (113 grams) unsalted butter, cubed and room temperature
- 2 teaspoons (10 grams) baking powder
- ½ teaspoon (1.5 grams) kosher salt

BUTTERCREAM:
- Swiss Meringue Buttercream (recipe on page 27)
- 2 teaspoons (8 grams) cotton candy flavoring, divided
- 2 to 3 drops blue gel food coloring
- 2 to 3 drops pink gel food coloring

Garnish: cotton candy, assorted sprinkles

**1.** Preheat oven to 350°F (180°C). Line a (12-cup) muffin pans with paper liners.

**2.** For the cupcakes: In a medium bowl, whisk together buttermilk, eggs, oil, cotton candy flavoring, and vanilla bean paste.

**3.** In the bowl of a stand mixer fitted with the paddle attachment, beat flour, sugar, butter, baking powder, and salt on medium speed until sandy texture and butter is fully incorporated. Add buttermilk mixture, and continue to beat until batter is well combined and smooth, 30 to 45 seconds. Scrape down sides and bottom of bowl. Continue to beat until batter is well combined and smooth, about 10 seconds. Divide batter among prepared muffin cups, filling each about three-fourths full.

**4.** Bake until a wooden pick inserted in center comes out clean, 20 to 25 minutes. Let cool in pans for 10 minutes. Remove from pans, and let cool completely on wire racks.

**5.** For the buttercream: Divide Swiss Meringue Buttercream between 2 medium bowls. Add 1 teaspoon (4 grams) cotton candy flavoring and blue food coloring to one bowl, and stir until well combined. Transfer to a 12-inch pastry bag.

**6.** To second bowl, add pink food coloring and remaining 1 teaspoon (13 grams) cotton candy flavoring, and stir until combined. Transfer to a 12-inch pastry bag. Cut tips off both pastry bags. Place both pastry bags in a 16-inch pastry bag fitted with your favorite piping tip. Pipe buttercream onto a plate until both mixtures are coming out. Pipe buttercream on top of cupcakes. Garnish with cotton candy and sprinkles, if desired.

# mom's lemon cake

MAKES 1 (13X9-INCH) CAKE

*My mom loves lemon cake, so I came up with a recipe that tastes like sunshine with each bite of soft cake and custardy lemon buttercream. This recipe is a heartfelt tribute to her, a symbol of gratitude and affection that will surely brighten her day.*

BUTTERCREAM:
- 1 cup (240 grams) whole milk
- 3 large egg yolks (57 grams)
- ¼ cup (50 grams) granulated sugar
- 3 tablespoons (24 grams) cornstarch
- ½ cup plus 2 tablespoons (141 grams) unsalted butter, room temperature and divided
- 1 teaspoon (4 grams) vanilla extract
- 1 teaspoon (4 grams) lemon extract (see note)
- ¼ teaspoon kosher salt
- 1 cup (120 grams) confectioners' sugar

CAKE:
- 3 cups (375 grams) all-purpose flour
- 1½ teaspoons (7.5 grams) baking powder
- ½ teaspoon (2.5 grams) baking soda
- ½ teaspoon (1.5 grams) kosher salt
- 2 cups (400 grams) granulated sugar
- 2 tablespoons (12 grams) lemon zest
- 1 cup (227 grams) salted butter, room temperature
- 3 large eggs (150 grams)
- 3 tablespoons (45 grams) fresh lemon juice
- 2 teaspoons (8 grams) lemon extract (see note)
- 1 teaspoon (4 grams) vanilla extract
- 1 cup (240 grams) sour cream, room temperature

**1.** For the buttercream: In a medium saucepan, heat milk over medium heat until an instant-read thermometer registers 150°F (66°C), 4 to 5 minutes. (Do not boil.)

**2.** In a large bowl, whisk together egg yolks, granulated sugar, and cornstarch until a smooth paste forms, 2 to 3 minutes. Slowly pour in warm milk, whisking constantly until combined. Pour mixture into saucepan. Bring to a boil; boil, whisking constantly, until mixture begins to thicken, 1 to 2 minutes. Remove from heat, and whisk for 1 minute. Add 1 tablespoon (14 grams) butter, extracts, and salt. Whisk until well combined. (If lumpy, press through a fine-mesh sieve.) Whisk for 1 minute to help assist in cooling. (Mixture should be very thick.) Transfer to large bowl. Cover with plastic wrap, pressing wrap directly onto surface of filling to prevent a film from forming. Refrigerate until cold, at least 2 hours. (If mixture is not cold enough, the frosting will be too loose.)

**3.** Meanwhile, for the cake: Preheat oven to 350°F (180°C). Using a pastry brush, brush a 13x9-inch baking dish with Cake Release (recipe on page 31) or spray with baking spray with flour. Line pan with parchment paper, letting excess extend over long sides of pan.

**4.** In a medium bowl, whisk together flour, baking powder, baking soda, and salt.

**5.** In a small bowl, using your fingers, pinch together granulated sugar and lemon zest until sugar is light yellow and fragrant.

**6.** In the bowl of a stand mixer fitted with the paddle attachment, beat butter on medium speed until smooth and creamy, about 2 minutes. Add lemon sugar, and continue to beat until fluffy and sugar is fully incorporated, about 3 minutes, scraping down sides of bowl. Add eggs, one at a time, ensuring each egg is fully incorporated prior to adding the next, about 15 seconds each. Scrape down sides and bottom of bowl. Continue to beat until well combined, about 1 minute. Add lemon juice and extracts; continue to beat until well combined, about 1 minute. With mixer on medium-low speed, gradually add flour mixture alternately with sour cream,

FAMILY FAVORITES

beginning and ending with flour mixture, beating until just combined after each addition. Pour batter into prepared pan.

**7.** Bake until a wooden pick inserted in center comes out clean, 35 to 40 minutes. Let cool in pan for 10 minutes. Using excess parchment as handles, remove from pan, and let cool completely on a wire rack.

**8.** Remove pastry cream from refrigerator, and whisk until smooth, 20 to 30 seconds. In the bowl of a stand mixer fitted with the whisk attachment, beat remaining ½ cup plus 1 tablespoon butter (127 grams) on high speed until fluffy and light in color, about 2 minutes. Add confectioners' sugar, and gradually increase mixer speed to high, beating until fluffy and smooth, about 30 seconds. Scrape down sides and bottom of bowl. With mixer on medium-high speed, add pastry cream, 2 tablespoons at a time, beating until there are no streaks left after each addition. Once all pastry cream is added, beat on high speed until smooth and fluffy, about 2 minutes. Using an offset spatula, spread buttercream onto cooled cake.

**NOTE:** *I love the flavor punch an emulsion or extract brings, but it can be a little much for some. If you prefer a less in-your-face flavor, omit the lemon extract.*

# dad's white chocolate and macadamia nut cookies

### MAKES ABOUT 15 LARGE COOKIES

*My dad's sweet tooth knows no bounds! From a young age, I can recall him sitting at the dining room table with a pack of cookies and going to town. I couldn't help but join in. Daddy and I would eat cookies and ice cream while watching the nightly news. White chocolate and macadamia cookies were always his favorite, so this recipe was inspired by those fond memories. They're like little bites of paradise! The creamy white chocolate chunks and crunchy macadamia nuts in each cookie create a balance of sweet and nutty that'll have you reaching for more. I took these to my Dad, and he 10,000% approves.*

| | |
|---|---|
| 2¼ | cups (281 grams) all-purpose flour |
| 1 | teaspoon (5 grams) baking soda |
| ½ | teaspoon (1.5 grams) kosher salt |
| ¾ | cup (170 grams) unsalted butter, room temperature |
| ¾ | cup (150 grams) granulated sugar |
| ½ | cup (110 grams) firmly packed light brown sugar |
| 1 | large egg (50 grams), room temperature |
| 1 | large egg yolk (19 grams), room temperature |
| 1 | tablespoon (18 grams) vanilla bean paste |
| 4.4 | ounces (124 grams) quality white chocolate, chopped |
| 1½ | cups (213 grams) macadamia nuts |

**1.** Preheat oven to 350°F (180°C). Line baking sheets with parchment paper.

**2.** In a large bowl, whisk together flour, baking soda, and salt.

**3.** In the bowl of a stand mixer fitted with the paddle attachment, beat butter on medium-low speed until creamy, about 2 minutes. Add sugars, and continue to beat until light and fluffy, about 2 minutes, scraping down sides of bowl. Add egg, egg yolk, and vanilla bean paste; continue to beat until all ingredients are well combined, about 1 minute. Scrape down sides of bowl. Reduce speed to low, and gradually add flour mixture, beating until just combined. Using a silicone spatula, fold in white chocolate and macadamia nuts.

**4.** Using a ¼-cup measuring cup, scoop dough, and roll each into a ball. Place dough balls 3 inches apart on prepared pans (3 to 4 per pan).

**5.** Bake, one pan at a time, until edges are set and centers are puffy, 10 to 12 minutes. To ensure the perfect circular cookie, place the open end of a large cup around edges of each cookie, swirling cup in a circular motion, making sure to touch edges with each movement. Let cool on pans for 10 minutes. Remove from pans, and let cool completely on a wire rack.

# hubby's giant blueberry breakfast pastry

**MAKES 12 SERVINGS**

*My husband LOVES breakfast pastries. I made this recipe for him during the COVID-19 pandemic when he couldn't find blueberry breakfast pastries in the store. He hasn't bought one since, which does wonders for my ego. This breakfast pastry is made with a flaky piecrust filled with wild blueberries. If blueberry is your jam or you just love more wholesome versions of nostalgic treats, you're going to love it.*

## FILLING:
- 3 cups (420 grams) frozen wild blueberries
- ¾ cup (150 grams) granulated sugar
- 2 tablespoons (30 grams) fresh lemon juice
- 2 tablespoons (16 grams) cornstarch
- 2 tablespoons (30 grams) water
- 2 tablespoons (28 grams) salted butter

## CRUST:
- 2½ cups (313 grams) all-purpose flour, plus more for dusting
- 2 tablespoons (24 grams) granulated sugar
- ½ teaspoon (1.5 grams) kosher salt
- ¾ cup (170 grams) cold salted butter, cubed
- 5 to 6 tablespoons (75 to 90 grams) cold whole milk

## EGG WASH:
- 1 large egg (50 grams)
- 1 tablespoon (15 grams) water

## GLAZE:
- 2 cups (240 grams) confectioners' sugar
- 2 to 3 tablespoons (30 to 45 grams) whole milk

1. For the filling: In a medium saucepan, combine blueberries, granulated sugar, and lemon juice. Bring to a boil over medium-high heat, stirring every 1 to 2 minutes. Boil, stirring frequently, for 5 minutes. Reduce heat to medium, and cook until mixture begins to thicken and bubble up, 15 to 20 minutes.
2. In a small bowl, stir together cornstarch and 2 tablespoons (30 grams) water. Add cornstarch slurry to blueberry mixture, and cook until thick, stirring frequently, 2 minutes. Remove from heat. Add butter, and stir until fully incorporated. Let cool completely.
3. For the crust: In a medium bowl, whisk together flour, granulated sugar, and salt. Add cold butter. Using your fingertips, toss and pinch butter into flour mixture until butter forms lima bean-size pieces. Add cold milk, 1 tablespoon at a time, mixing until dough comes together but isn't wet and sticky.
4. Turn out dough onto a lightly floured surface, and press together to shape into a square. Divide dough in half, and wrap each half in plastic wrap. Refrigerate for at least 30 minutes.
5. For the egg wash: In a small bowl, whisk together egg and 1 tablespoon (15 grams) water.
6. Line an 18x13-inch baking sheet with parchment paper.
7. Place half of dough on a lightly floured surface. Using a rolling pin, roll dough into a 13x9-inch rectangle. Transfer dough to prepared pan. Reserve ¼ cup (80 grams) filling for glaze; spread remaining filling on top, leaving a 1-inch border around edges. Using a pastry brush, brush edges of dough with egg wash.
8. On a lightly floured surface, roll remaining dough into a 13x9-inch rectangle. Place on top of filling. Using a fork, crimp edges of dough to seal crusts and then poke holes 2 inches apart on top. Trim excess dough to create clean edges if desired. Freeze for 20 minutes.
9. Position oven rack in bottom third of oven. Preheat oven to 375°F (190°C).
10. Lightly brush top of dough with egg wash.
11. Bake until golden brown, 22 to 25 minutes. Let cool completely on pan.
12. For the glaze: In a large bowl, whisk together reserved ¼ cup (80 grams) filling and confectioners' sugar until combined. Add milk, 1 tablespoon (15 grams) at a time, whisking until it reaches desired consistency. Pour glaze on top of pastry.

# mom's midnight cookie crunch

**MAKES 10 TO 12 SERVINGS**

*My mom has been making this every holiday for as long as I can remember. It's crushed chocolate cookies with a luscious, whipped cream. It's just divine, yet so simple to make. I tip my hat to my mom on this one. It's my favorite dessert of all time.*

40  cream-filled chocolate sandwich cookies* (453 grams)

CREAM:
- 2 (3.4-ounce) packages (192 grams) vanilla instant pudding mix
- 3½ cups (840 grams) whole milk
- 1 (8-ounce) package (226 grams) cream cheese, room temperature
- 1½ cups (180 grams) confectioners' sugar
- ½ cup (113 grams) unsalted butter, room temperature
- 2 teaspoons (8 grams) vanilla extract
- 1 (16-ounce) container (453 grams) frozen whipped topping, thawed

TOPPING:
- 1 tablespoon (15 grams) fresh lemon juice
- 6 large egg whites (180 grams)
- ¾ cup (150 grams) granulated sugar
- ½ teaspoon (1.5 grams) cream of tartar
- 1 teaspoon (4 grams) vanilla extract
- Pinch kosher salt

**1.** Open each sandwich cookie, and scrape off cream filling. Discard filling or reserve for another use. Place cookies in the container of a food processor, and pulse until texture resembles sand and uniform crumbles form.

**2.** For the cream: In a large bowl, beat pudding mixes and milk with a handheld mixer on medium speed until smooth.

**3.** In another large bowl, using clean beaters, beat cream cheese, confectioners' sugar, butter, and vanilla extract with a handheld mixer on medium speed until smooth and fully combined. Add cream cheese mixture to pudding mixture, and beat on medium speed until all lumps are gone and mixture is fluffy and smooth. Fold in whipped topping until well incorporated.

**4.** In a trifle bowl or a large serving bowl, spoon one-half of cream mixture. Layer one-half of crushed cookies on top. Repeat layers with remaining cream mixture and remaining crushed cookies.

**5.** For topping: In the bowl of a stand mixer, place lemon juice. Using a paper towel, wipe down sides and bottom of bowl with lemon juice until nothing remains. (This will help remove any oils and excess moisture from the bowl.) Let dry.

**6.** In the top of a double boiler, whisk together egg whites and granulated sugar. Cook over simmering water, whisking frequently, until sugar fully dissolves and an instant-read thermometer registers 150°F (65°C). (Sugar is dissolved when you can rub the mixture between your fingers and feel no sugar.)

**7.** Transfer egg white mixture to the cleaned bowl of a stand mixer fitted with the whisk attachment. Beat on low speed, increasing mixer speed to medium as mixture becomes bubbly. Add cream of tartar, and continue to beat until stiff peaks form and meringue is glossy and white, 7 to 10 minutes. Add vanilla extract and salt, beating until fully combined, about 1 minute. Spoon topping onto trifle. Using a handheld kitchen torch, carefully brown topping.

*\*I use Oreos.*

# jayna's snickerdoodle cheesecake
## WITH COOKIE WHIPPED CREAM

### MAKES 1 (9-INCH) CHEESECAKE

*I met my best friend in Boston Logan International Airport in 2013. As I opened a bag of chips, a chip popped out of the bag and smacked her in the face. I apologized, and we've been best friends since. Her favorite food is cheesecake, so when she visited for Thanksgiving one year, I decided to make her this recipe. On Thanksgiving morning, we sat in our PJ's having mimosas and this cheesecake for breakfast. This memory always makes me smile. The cheesecake has a creamy cinnamon-sugar filling and is topped with a cookie whipped cream that makes this recipe truly stand out.*

CRUST:
- 14 sheets cinnamon graham crackers (210 grams)
- 6 tablespoons (84 grams) salted butter, melted
- ¼ cup (50 grams) granulated sugar
- ½ teaspoon (1 gram) ground cinnamon
- Pinch kosher salt

FILLING:
- 4 (8-ounce) packages (907 grams) cream cheese, room temperature
- 1½ cups (300 grams) granulated sugar
- 4 large eggs (200 grams), room temperature
- ½ cup (120 grams) sour cream, room temperature
- 1 tablespoon (6 grams) ground cinnamon
- 1 tablespoon (13 grams) vanilla extract
- Boiling water

WHIPPED CREAM:
- 2 cups (480 grams) cold heavy whipping cream
- ½ cup (60 grams) confectioners' sugar
- 4 to 6 snickerdoodle cookies*, finely crushed (about 1 cup)

Garnish: snickerdoodle cookie crumbs

1. Preheat oven to 325°F (170°C). Wrap bottom and sides of a 9-inch springform pan in heavy-duty foil.

2. For the crust: In the work bowl of a food processor, process graham crackers until uniform and fine. Add melted butter, granulated sugar, cinnamon, and salt; process until all ingredients are combined and mixture starts to stick together. Pour into prepared pan, and using a cup, press mixture into bottom of pan. Refrigerate until ready to use.

3. For the filling: In the bowl of a stand mixer fitted with the paddle attachment, place cream cheese and granulated sugar; gradually increase mixer speed to medium, beating until smooth and sugar dissolves. Add eggs, one at a time, ensuring each egg is fully incorporated prior to adding the next, scraping down sides of bowl. Beat in sour cream, cinnamon, and vanilla extract, scraping down sides of bowl. Continue to beat for 5 minutes, scraping down sides of bowl to make sure everything is well combined. Pour into pan on top of prepared crust.

4. Carefully place springform pan in a large roasting pan. Place roasting pan in oven. Pour boiling water into roasting pan until water covers the bottom 1 to 2 inches of springform pan.

5. Bake until edges are set but center is still jiggly, 1 hour and 40 minutes to 1 hour and 50 minutes. Carefully remove cheesecake from water bath, and let cool completely in pan on a wire rack, 1 to 2 hours. (Once pan is cool enough to handle, carefully remove foil from sides.) Refrigerate in pan on a wire rack overnight, loosely covering with foil only when completely cool to prevent condensation from forming on top of cheesecake.

6. For the whipped cream: In the bowl of a stand mixer fitted with the whisk attachment, beat cold cream and confectioners' sugar on medium speed until stiff peaks form. Fold in crushed cookies. Place in a pastry bag fitted with your favorite piping tip.

7. Carefully remove chilled cheesecake from pan, and transfer to a serving plate. Pipe whipped cream on top as desired. Garnish with cookie crumbs, if desired. Use a warm, dry knife to slice when ready to serve.

*You can use store-bought cookies, or I like to use Pillsbury Sugar Cookie Dough with 1 tablespoon (6 grams) ground cinnamon mixed in and then baked according to package directions and cooled. Cookies are processed in a food processor until uniform and fine.

# rowan's lemon-blueberry bars

**MAKES 9 BARS**

*My baby boy LOVES to eat. When I was testing this recipe, my mom called me. I was on the phone with her for about two minutes when I realized my son pulled the stepping stool over to the counter, grabbed a piece of the lemon bars, and rammed it into his mouth. I couldn't help but laugh when he said, "Mommy, this is good, more please." He loved them so much, I had to dedicate this recipe to him, my bright-eyed baby boy. The delightful fusion of tangy lemon and bursting blueberries match his zest for life. May these bars not only tantalize your senses but also fill your heart with warmth and joy, just as they do for me every time I bake them.*

**CRUST:**
- 1½ cups (188 grams) all-purpose flour
- ½ cup (100 grams) granulated sugar
- ½ teaspoon (1.5 grams) kosher salt
- ½ cup (113 grams) salted butter, room temperature

**FILLING:**
- 2 (14-ounce) cans (792 grams) sweetened condensed milk
- 6 large egg yolks (114 grams), room temperature
- 1 tablespoon (6 grams) lemon zest
- ¾ cup (180 grams) fresh lemon juice
- 1 teaspoon (4 grams) lemon extract

**TOPPING:**
- 1¼ cups (187 grams) fresh blueberries, plus more to decorate
- ¼ cup (60 grams) heavy whipping cream
- 13.2 ounces (375 grams) quality white chocolate, chopped
- 2½ tablespoons (15 grams) ground freeze-dried blueberries, sifted
- 2 tablespoons (28 grams) unsalted butter, room temperature

1. Preheat oven to 350°F (180°C). Line an 8-inch square baking pan with parchment paper, letting excess extend by 2 inches over all sides of pan.
2. For the crust: In a large bowl, whisk together flour, sugar, and salt. Using your hands, cut in butter until mixture is crumbly and butter is fully incorporated. (You should be able to squeeze the crust in your hand and have it stick together.) Press dough evenly into bottom and halfway up sides of prepared pan.
3. Bake until edges are slightly golden and puffy, 15 to 20 minutes. Let cool for 20 minutes. Leave oven on.
4. For the filling: In a medium bowl, whisk together condensed milk, egg yolks, and lemon zest until smooth, about 1 minute. Add lemon juice and lemon extract. Whisk until smooth. Pour into prepared crust.
5. Bake until edges are set but center is slightly jiggly, 20 to 25 minutes. Let cool for 1 hour.
6. For the topping: In the work bowl of a food processor, process fresh blueberries on high until smooth. Place a fine-mesh sieve over a large bowl. Press blueberries through sieve, collecting the juice. (You'll need ¼ cup or 60 grams juice. If your blueberries yield more, save for another recipe.)
7. In a small saucepan, heat blueberry juice and cream over low heat until heated through, 3 to 4 minutes. Add white chocolate. Gently stir until white chocolate is fully melted. Remove from heat, and stir in ground blueberries and butter until fully incorporated. Pour on top of filling. Top with additional blueberries. Refrigerate until set, at least 2 hours. Using excess parchment as handles, remove from pan, and cut into bars.

# classic vanilla pound cake

MAKES 1 (15-CUP) BUNDT CAKE

*There's something special about a classic vanilla pound cake with a golden-brown crust that gives way to a tender, buttery crumb. My favorite way to enjoy it is with some fresh berries and a scoop of ice cream. Once you try it, you'll understand why it never goes out of style.*

CAKE:
- 3 cups (600 grams) plus 2 tablespoons (24 grams) granulated sugar, divided
- 1 cup (227 grams) unsalted butter, room temperature
- 1 (8-ounce) package (226 grams) cream cheese, room temperature
- 7 large eggs (350 grams), room temperature
- 1½ tablespoons (27 grams) vanilla bean paste
- 3 cups (375 grams) all-purpose flour
- 1 teaspoon (3 grams) kosher salt

GLAZE:
- 2½ cups (300 grams) confectioners' sugar
- 2 to 4 tablespoons (30 to 60 grams) whole milk
- 2 tablespoons (28 grams) unsalted butter, melted

1. For the cake: Preheat oven to 325°F (170°C). Using a pastry brush, brush a 15-cup Bundt pan with Cake Release (recipe on page 31) or spray with baking spray with flour. Sprinkle 2 tablespoons (24 grams) granulated sugar in pan, swirling to coat. Tap out any excess.

2. In the bowl of a stand mixer fitted with the paddle attachment, beat butter and cream cheese on medium-low speed until smooth and well combined, about 3 minutes. Add remaining 3 cups (600 grams) granulated sugar, and continue to beat until fluffy, about 5 minutes, scraping down sides of bowl. Add eggs, one at a time, ensuring each egg is fully incorporated prior to adding the next, frequently scraping down sides of bowl. Beat in vanilla bean paste. Add flour and salt, and beat on low speed until just combined, scraping down sides of bowl. Spoon batter into prepared pan, smoothing top.

3. Bake until a wooden pick inserted near center comes out clean or with just a few moist crumbs, 1 hour and 10 minutes to 1 hour and 20 minutes. Let cool in pan on a wire rack for 10 minutes. Invert cake onto a wire rack, and let cool completely.

4. For the glaze: In a medium bowl, whisk together all ingredients until smooth and desired consistency is reached. Drizzle on top of cooled cake.

# sweet potato pie

### MAKES 1 (9-INCH) PIE

*Gather round for a slice of my family's cherished Sweet Potato Pie. Picture a golden, flaky crust cradling a lush filling made from creamy sweet potatoes, infused with warm spices, and kissed with a hint of vanilla. This is sure to become a treasured favorite in your own family for years to come.*

**CRUST:**
- 1½ cups (188 grams) all-purpose flour, plus more for dusting
- 2 tablespoons (24 grams) granulated sugar
- ½ teaspoon (1 gram) ground cinnamon
- ¼ teaspoon kosher salt
- ¼ teaspoon ground nutmeg
- ½ cup (113 grams) cold salted butter, cubed
- ¼ cup (60 grams) ice water

**FILLING:**
- 3 large sweet potatoes (about 730 grams)
- 1 cup (220 grams) firmly packed light brown sugar
- 6 tablespoons (88 grams) Browned Butter (recipe on page 28), cooled
- ⅓ cup (80 grams) evaporated milk
- ¼ cup (50 grams) granulated sugar
- 1 tablespoon (6 grams) ground cinnamon
- ½ teaspoon (1 gram) ground ginger
- ¼ teaspoon kosher salt
- ¼ teaspoon ground nutmeg
- ¼ teaspoon ground cloves
- ¼ cup (31 grams) all-purpose flour
- 3 large eggs (150 grams), room temperature
- 1 tablespoon (13 grams) vanilla extract

**MERINGUE:**
- 3 large egg whites (90 grams)
- 6 tablespoons (84 grams) firmly packed light brown sugar
- ¼ teaspoon cream of tartar
- ½ teaspoon (2 grams) vanilla extract
- Pinch kosher salt

1. Preheat oven to 425°F (220°C). Line a baking sheet with parchment paper.
2. For the crust: In a large bowl, whisk together flour, granulated sugar, cinnamon, salt, and nutmeg. Add cold butter, and pinch together until butter is fully incorporated into flour and pea-size pieces remain. Make a well in center; add ¼ cup (60 grams) ice water, 1 to 2 tablespoons (15 to 30 grams) at a time, stirring until a shaggy dough forms.
3. Turn out dough onto a lightly floured surface, and press any scraps together to form one cohesive dough. Wrap in plastic wrap, and refrigerate for 1 hour.
4. Meanwhile, for the filling: Rinse and dry sweet potatoes. Place on prepared pan.
5. Bake until soft and easily pierced with a fork, 30 to 45 minutes. Let cool enough to handle.
6. Remove potato skin, and place potato flesh in a large bowl. Let cool completely, 1 to 2 hours.
7. Mash potatoes. (Be sure to remove any stringy fibers.) (Optional: Press mashed potato through a fine-mesh sieve to remove any lumps and residual stringy fibers.)
8. In a large bowl, stir together sweet potatoes, brown sugar, Browned Butter, evaporated milk, granulated sugar, cinnamon, ginger, salt, nutmeg, and cloves until combined. Add flour, eggs, and vanilla extract, and mash with a potato masher until eggs are fully incorporated.
9. On a lightly floured surface, roll crust dough into a 10-inch circle (about ¼ inch thick). Transfer dough to a 9-inch pie pan, pressing into bottom and up sides.

Trim excess dough to ½ inch beyond edge of pan. Fold edges under, and crimp as desired. Freeze for 20 minutes.

10. Position oven rack in bottom third of oven. Preheat oven to 425°F (220°C).

11. Dock bottom of crust so air bubbles do not form while baking. Top crust with a piece of parchment paper, letting ends extend over edges of pan. Add pie weights.

12. Bake until edges are golden brown, 10 to 15 minutes. Carefully remove parchment and weights, and bake until bottom of crust is golden brown, 10 to 13 minutes more. Reduce oven temperature to 350°F (180°C).

13. Add filling to prepared crust, and cover edges of crust with foil to prevent burning.

14. Bake until center of pie is slightly jiggly, 35 to 40 minutes. Let cool completely on a wire rack.

15. For the meringue: In the bowl of a stand mixer, place lemon juice. Using a paper towel, wipe down sides and bottom of bowl with lemon juice until nothing remains. (This will help remove any oils and excess moisture from the bowl.) Let dry. In the top of a double boiler, whisk together egg whites and sugar. Cook over simmering water, stirring occasionally, until sugar fully dissolves and an instant-read thermometer registers 150°F (66°C), 5 to 7 minutes. (Sugar is dissolved when you can rub the mixture between your fingers and feel no sugar.)

16. In the cleaned bowl of a stand mixer fitted with the whisk attachment, carefully place egg mixture. Beat on low speed until bubbly. Add cream of tartar and beat on medium speed until stiff peaks form and meringue is glossy and white, 7 to 10 minutes. Add vanilla extract and salt, and whisk until just combined. Transfer to a 12-inch pastry bag fitted with your favorite piping tip. Pipe on top of cooled pie as desired. Using a handheld kitchen torch, carefully brown meringue.

**TIPS**

*To save time, you can use a store-bought piecrust. You'll want to get a 9-inch piecrust, so keep that in mind.*

*For best results, I recommend using fresh sweet potatoes for this recipe as opposed to canned sweet potato purée. The canned purée tends to have more water in it, which prevents the filling from thickening up while baking.*

*Make sure that the pie weights completely fill the pie pan to the top of the crust. You can also use uncooked rice or uncooked beans. Just don't cook and eat them after.*

*Add the topping only after the pie has cooled completely. If the pie is warm, the meringue will melt.*

# salted honey mille-feuilles

MAKES 6 MILLE-FEUILLES

*This recipe is inspired by a little Parisian pâtisserie I stumbled upon during one of my many visits to the City of Light. I ordered my first mille-feuille there, and I was so in love that I had to make my own. The layers of crisp, flaky pastry are generously filled with a luscious salted honey pastry cream that's the perfect balance of sweet and salty. It's truly exquisite and will transport you to the enchanting streets of Paris with every indulgent bite. Bon appétit!*

- 2 cups (480 grams) whole milk
- ¼ cup (85 grams) honey, plus more to serve
- 5 large egg yolks (95 grams)
- ⅓ cup (67 grams) granulated sugar
- 4 tablespoons (32 grams) cornstarch
- 2 tablespoons (28 grams) salted butter
- 2 teaspoons (12 grams) vanilla bean paste
- ¼ teaspoon kosher salt
- All-purpose flour, for dusting
- ½ (17.3-ounce) package (245 grams) frozen puff pastry (1 sheet), thawed according to package directions

**1.** In a medium saucepan, heat milk and honey over low heat until simmering and warmed throughout (about 105°F/41°C), 5 to 7 minutes.

**2.** In a medium bowl, whisk together egg yolks, sugar, and cornstarch until a thick paste forms. Slowly add warm milk mixture, about ½ cup (120 grams) at a time, whisking constantly to prevent egg yolks from cooking. Once all milk mixture is added, pour mixture back into the saucepan. Increase heat to medium, and bring to a boil, whisking constantly. Remove from heat, and whisk vigorously for 1 minute. Add butter, vanilla bean paste, and salt, whisking until butter is fully melted. Strain through a fine-mesh sieve into a large bowl. Cover with plastic wrap, pressing wrap directly onto surface of pastry cream to prevent a film from forming. Refrigerate until set, about 2 hours.

**3.** Preheat oven to 400°F (200°C). Line a baking sheet with parchment paper.

**4.** On a well-floured surface, roll puff pastry sheet to about ⅛-inch thickness. Using a sharp knife, cut pastry into 18 (4x2-inch) rectangles. Place 10 pastry rectangles on prepared pan. Place another piece of parchment paper on top. Place another baking sheet on top of pastry to weigh down.

**5.** Bake for 8 minutes. Rotate pan, and bake for 7 minutes more. Remove from pan, and let cool completely on a wire rack. Repeat procedure with remaining 8 pastry rectangles.

**6.** Using a serrated knife, gently trim sides of cooled pastry rectangles. (This will expose the flaky layers.)

**7.** Whisk cooled pastry cream until smooth. Place in a pastry bag fitted with your favorite piping tip. Pipe pastry cream on top of pastry rectangles.

**8.** Place 1 pastry rectangle on a plate, and stack 2 more rectangles on top, creating 1 (3-layer) mille-feuille. Repeat with remaining rectangles. Drizzle with honey to serve, if desired.

# ashley's vanilla bean cheesecake

**MAKES 1 (9-INCH) CHEESECAKE**

*Indulgent, timeless, elegant—this luxurious Vanilla Bean Cheesecake is everything you want in a dessert. Whether you're hosting a special occasion or simply craving a sweet escape, prepare to elevate your dessert game to new heights with this classic favorite.*

CRUST:
- 10 tablespoons (130 grams) Browned Butter (recipe on page 28), melted
- 18 graham cracker sheets (270 grams)
- ¼ cup (50 grams) granulated sugar
- ¼ teaspoon ground nutmeg
- Pinch kosher salt

FILLING:
- 4 (8-ounce) packages (907 grams) cream cheese, room temperature
- 1½ cups (300 grams) granulated sugar
- 2 tablespoons (16 grams) cornstarch
- 1½ tablespoons (27 grams) vanilla bean paste
- 4 large eggs (200 grams), room temperature
- ¾ cup (180 grams) sour cream, room temperature
- ½ cup (120 grams) heavy whipping cream, room temperature
- 2 tablespoons (30 grams) bourbon
- ¼ teaspoon kosher salt
- ⅛ teaspoon ground nutmeg

Boiling water

TOPPING:
- 1½ cups (360 grams) cold heavy whipping cream
- ⅓ cup (40 grams) confectioners' sugar
- 2 teaspoons (12 grams) vanilla bean paste

Garnish: white chocolate shavings

**1.** Preheat oven to 350°F (180°C). Line a 9-inch springform pan with parchment paper. Wrap bottom and sides of a 9-inch springform pan in heavy-duty foil.

**2.** For the crust: In the bowl of a food processor, process graham crackers, granulated sugar, nutmeg, and salt until fine, uniform crumbs form. With food processor running, add melted Browned Butter. Stop and scrape down sides of bowl. Continue to process until texture resembles wet sand, about 1 minute. Using the bottom of a cup, press crumb mixture into bottom and up sides of prepared pan.

**3.** Bake until set and fragrant, about 12 minutes. Let cool completely. Reduce oven temperature to 325°F (170°C).

**4.** For the filling: In the bowl of a stand mixer fitted with the paddle attachment, beat cream cheese on low speed for 3 minutes. Add granulated sugar, cornstarch, vanilla bean paste, and reserved browned butter bits; continue to beat for 2 minutes. Scrape down sides of bowl. Add eggs, one at a time, ensuring each egg is fully incorporated prior to adding the next. Scrape down sides of bowl. Add sour cream, cream, bourbon, salt, and nutmeg, and continue to beat for 2 minutes. Pour batter into cooled prepared crust in pan.

**5.** Carefully place springform pan in a large roasting pan. Place roasting pan in oven. Pour boiling water into roasting pan until water covers the bottom 1 to 2 inches of springform pan.

**6.** Bake until edges are set and center is still jiggly, about 1 hour and 20 minutes. Carefully remove cheesecake from water bath, and let cool completely in pan on a wire rack, 1 to 2 hours. (Once pan is cool enough to handle, carefully remove foil from sides.) Refrigerate in pan on a wire rack overnight, loosely covering with foil only when completely cool to prevent condensation from forming on top of cheesecake.

**7.** For the topping: In a large bowl, beat cold cream and confectioners' sugar with a handheld mixer on medium speed until stiff peaks form, about 5 minutes. Fold in vanilla bean paste.

**8.** Remove cheesecake from pan, and dollop topping on top of cheesecake. Garnish with white chocolate, if desired.

# *the cornbread*
## THAT EVERYONE ASKS ME TO MAKE OVER AND OVER AGAIN

**MAKES 1 (9-INCH) LOAF**

*Oh, how I love this recipe! Every time I make it, folks rave about it. It's moist, buttery, sweet, and goes well with a big pot of chili, or simply slathered in butter by itself. Whatever you do, don't take this to a party unless you are ready to make it over and over again.*

| | |
|---|---|
| 1 | cup (240 grams) whole buttermilk, room temperature |
| ¾ | cup (170 grams) unsalted butter, melted |
| ¼ | cup (50 grams) granulated sugar |
| ¼ | cup (55 grams) firmly packed light brown sugar |
| ¼ | cup (60 grams) sour cream, room temperature |
| 2 | tablespoons (28 grams) vegetable oil |
| 1 | (3.4-ounce) package (96 grams) vanilla instant pudding mix |
| 1 | teaspoon (4 grams) vanilla extract |
| 2 | large eggs (100 grams), room temperature |
| 1¼ | cups (156 grams) all-purpose flour |
| 1 | cup (150 grams) medium-grind yellow cornmeal* |
| 2 | teaspoons (10 grams) baking powder |
| ½ | teaspoon (2.5 grams) baking soda |
| ½ | teaspoon (1.5 grams) kosher salt |

Softened salted butter, to serve

**1.** Preheat oven to 350°F (180°C). Spray a 9-inch cast-iron skillet or a 9-inch round cake pan with cooking spray.

**2.** In a large bowl, whisk together buttermilk, melted butter, sugars, sour cream, and oil. Add pudding mix and vanilla extract, and whisk until well combined. Add eggs, one at a time, ensuring each egg is fully incorporated prior to adding the next.

**3.** In a medium bowl, whisk together flour, cornmeal, baking powder, baking soda, and salt. Add flour mixture to buttermilk mixture, folding until just combined. Pour into prepared skillet or pan.

**4.** Bake until golden brown and a wooden pick inserted in center comes out clean, 35 to 40 minutes (for cast-iron skillet) or 45 to 50 minutes (for cake pan). Let cool in skillet or pan for 5 to 10 minutes. Serve with softened salted butter.

*I use Bob's Red Mill Medium Grind Yellow Cornmeal.

# autumn delights

# apple cider doughnut bars

MAKES ABOUT 16 DOUGHNUTS

*With the charm of classic doughnuts and the ease of a bar dessert, these treats are infused with concentrated apple cider, delivering a burst of orchard-fresh flavor in every bite.*

DOUGHNUTS:
- 2 cups (480 grams) apple cider
- ¾ cup (94 grams) all-purpose flour
- ¾ cup (72 grams) almond flour
- 2 teaspoons (4 grams) ground cinnamon
- ¼ teaspoon ground allspice
- ⅛ teaspoon kosher salt
- 5 large egg whites (150 grams), room temperature
- ½ cup (100 grams) granulated sugar
- ½ cup (104 grams) Browned Butter (recipe on page 28), room temperature
- 1 teaspoon (6 grams) vanilla bean paste

COATING:
- ¾ cup (150 grams) granulated sugar
- 1½ teaspoons (3 grams) ground cinnamon
- ¼ teaspoon ground ginger
- ⅛ teaspoon ground allspice

1. For the doughnuts: In a medium saucepan, heat apple cider over high heat, stirring frequently, until reduced to ¼ cup, 20 to 25 minutes. Pour cider into a heatproof container, and refrigerate until completely cooled and thickened (see note), about 50 minutes.
2. In a large bowl, whisk together flours, cinnamon, allspice, and salt.
3. In another large bowl, whisk together egg whites and sugar until bubbly, about 3 minutes. Whisk in reduced cider, Browned Butter, and vanilla bean paste until fully combined. Fold in flour mixture until just combined. Transfer batter to a 12-inch pastry bag, and refrigerate for 1 hour.
4. Preheat oven to 350°F (180°C). Using a pastry brush, brush 2 (8-well) financier pans with Cake Release (recipe on page 31) or spray with baking spray with flour. (If using a nonstick financier pan, no need to spray.)
5. For the coating: In a small bowl, whisk together all ingredients.
6. Trim and transfer filled pastry bag to a large pastry bag fitted with a medium round piping tip. Pipe batter into prepared pan, filling each mold about three-fourths full.
7. Bake until golden brown and a wooden pick inserted in center comes out clean, 15 to 17 minutes. Immediately remove from pans and toss in coating.

NOTE: *When completely cooled, the apple cider reduction should be as thick as jam.*

# *pumpkin bread*
## WITH CINNAMON STREUSEL AND BUTTERY MAPLE GLAZE

**MAKES 1 (9X5-INCH) LOAF**

*A rich, spiced bread is topped with a flavorful streusel and drizzled with a buttery maple glaze. As the glaze glides into every nook and cranny, you're greeted with a harmonious blend of sweet, spiced, and buttery flavors that warm the heart and soul.*

**STREUSEL:**
- ¼ cup (55 grams) firmly packed light brown sugar
- ⅓ cup plus 1 tablespoon (50 grams) all-purpose flour
- ½ teaspoon (1 gram) ground cinnamon
- Pinch kosher salt
- 2 tablespoons (28 grams) unsalted butter, melted

**BREAD:**
- 2 cups (250 grams) all-purpose flour
- 1 tablespoon (6 grams) ground cinnamon
- 1 teaspoon (5 grams) baking soda
- 1 teaspoon (2 grams) ground ginger
- 1 teaspoon (2 grams) ground allspice
- ½ teaspoon (1.5 grams) kosher salt
- ½ teaspoon (1 gram) ground nutmeg
- ½ teaspoon (1 gram) ground cloves
- 1 (15-ounce) can (425 grams) pumpkin purée
- 1 cup (220 grams) firmly packed light brown sugar
- ¾ cup (150 grams) granulated sugar
- ¼ cup (57 grams) unsalted butter, melted
- ¼ cup (57 grams) vegetable oil
- 2 large eggs (100 grams), room temperature
- ¼ cup (60 grams) sour cream, room temperature
- 1 teaspoon (4 grams) vanilla extract

**GLAZE:**
- 1 cup (120 grams) confectioners' sugar
- ¼ cup (57 grams) unsalted butter, melted
- 2 tablespoons (42 grams) maple syrup
- 1 to 2 tablespoons (15 to 30 grams) heavy whipping cream
- 1 teaspoon (4 grams) vanilla extract

**1.** Preheat oven to 350°F (180°C). Line a 9x5-inch loaf pan with parchment paper, letting excess extend by 1 inch over all sides of pan.

**2.** For the streusel: In a medium bowl, stir together brown sugar, flour, cinnamon, and salt. Add melted butter. Stir until small crumbles form. Cover and refrigerate until ready to use.

**3.** For the bread: In a medium bowl, whisk together flour, cinnamon, baking soda, ginger, allspice, salt, nutmeg, and cloves.

**4.** In a large bowl, whisk together pumpkin, brown sugar, granulated sugar, melted butter, and oil until sugars begin to dissolve, 2 to 3 minutes. Add eggs, and whisk until fully combined. Add sour cream and vanilla extract, and whisk until fully combined. Using a silicone spatula, fold in flour mixture until just combined and no dry streaks remain. Pour batter into prepared pan. Top with streusel.

**5.** Bake until a wooden pick inserted in center comes out with just a few crumbs, 1 hour and 20 minutes to 1½ hours. Let cool in pan for 30 minutes.

**6.** For the glaze: In a medium bowl, whisk together all ingredients. Drizzle on top of bread.

# churro bundt cake

MAKES 1 (12-CUP) BUNDT CAKE

*The espresso-infused cinnamon sugar coating on this moist Bundt cakes adds a crunchy texture and a hint of coffee flavor, reminiscent of the beloved coating on classic churros. With each slice, you'll delight in a heavenly blend of sweet and robust flavors.*

CAKE:
- 2¾ cups (550 grams) plus 2 tablespoons (24 grams) granulated sugar, divided
- 3 cups (375 grams) all-purpose flour
- 2 teaspoons (4 grams) ground cinnamon
- 1 teaspoon (3 grams) kosher salt
- ½ teaspoon (1 gram) ground nutmeg
- 1½ cups (340 grams) unsalted butter, room temperature
- 1 (8-ounce) package (226 grams) cream cheese, room temperature
- 6 large eggs (300 grams), room temperature
- 1 tablespoon (13 grams) vanilla extract

COATING:
- ¼ cup (50 grams) granulated sugar
- 1½ teaspoons (3 grams) ground cinnamon
- ¾ teaspoon (1.5 grams) espresso powder
- 2 tablespoons (28 grams) unsalted butter, melted

1. For the cake: Preheat oven to 325°F (170°C). Using a pastry brush, brush a 12-cup Bundt pan with Cake Release (recipe on page 31) or spray with baking spray with flour. Sprinkle 2 tablespoons (24 grams) granulated sugar in pan, swirling to coat. Tap out any excess.

2. In a medium bowl, whisk together flour, cinnamon, salt, and nutmeg.

3. In the bowl of a stand mixer fitted with the paddle attachment, beat butter and cream cheese on medium-low speed for 1 minute. Add remaining 2¾ cups (550 grams) sugar, and continue to beat until fluffy, about 4 minutes. Scrape down sides and bottom of bowl with a silicone spatula. Add eggs, one at a time, ensuring each egg is fully incorporated prior to adding the next, about 15 seconds each, scraping down sides and bottom of bowl after fourth egg and sixth egg. Add flour mixture and vanilla extract, gradually increasing mixer speed to medium. Scrape down sides and bottom of bowl. Beat at medium speed until well combined, 15 to 20 seconds. Spoon batter into prepared pan.

4. Bake until golden brown and a wooden pick inserted near center comes out clean, 1 hour and 25 minutes to 1½ hours. Let cool in pan for 10 minutes. Invert cake onto a wire rack, and unmold from pan. Let cool completely.

5. For the coating: In a small bowl, whisk together sugar, cinnamon, and espresso powder.

6. Brush outside of cooled cake with melted butter. Sprinkle with sugar mixture to coat.

# sweet potato-carrot cake

MAKES 1 (8-INCH) CAKE

*For more than two years, I have been waiting for a special moment to share this recipe. What's more special than my first cookbook? The sweet potatoes give this cake an incredibly moist texture, offering a rich depth of flavor that's balanced by a velvety cream cheese frosting. Each bite is a comforting blend of warm spices and sweet, creamy goodness!*

CAKE:
- 1 pound (455 grams) sweet potatoes
- 2¾ cups (344 grams) all-purpose flour
- 1 tablespoon (6 grams) ground cinnamon
- 2 teaspoons (10 grams) baking powder
- 1 teaspoon (5 grams) baking soda
- 1 teaspoon (3 grams) kosher salt
- 1 teaspoon (2 grams) ground ginger
- ½ teaspoon (1 gram) ground nutmeg
- ¼ teaspoon ground cloves
- ¼ teaspoon ground allspice
- ½ cup (113 grams) unsalted butter, room temperature
- 1 cup (200 grams) granulated sugar
- 1 cup (220 grams) firmly packed light brown sugar
- ½ cup (112 grams) vegetable oil
- 4 large eggs (200 grams), room temperature
- 2 teaspoons (8 grams) vanilla extract
- 2½ cups (325 grams) shredded carrot

FROSTING:
- ¾ cup (170 grams) unsalted butter, room temperature
- 12 ounces (340 grams) cream cheese, room temperature
- 5 cups (600 grams) confectioners' sugar
- 1 tablespoon (10 grams) meringue powder
- 1 teaspoon (4 grams) vanilla extract
- Pinch kosher salt

1. Preheat oven to 425°F (220°C). Line a baking sheet with parchment paper.
2. For the cake: Rinse and dry sweet potatoes. Place on prepared pan.
3. Bake until soft and easily pierced with a fork, 30 to 45 minutes. Let cool enough to handle.
4. Remove skin, and place potato flesh in a large bowl. Let cool completely, 1 to 2 hours. Mash potatoes.
5. Preheat oven to 350°F (180°C). Using a pastry brush, brush 3 (8-inch) round cake pans with Cake Release (recipe on page 31) or spray with baking spray with flour.
6. In a large bowl, whisk together flour, cinnamon, baking powder, baking soda, salt, ginger, nutmeg, cloves, and allspice.
7. In the bowl of a stand mixer fitted with the paddle attachment, beat butter, granulated sugar, brown sugar, and oil on medium speed until well combined and smooth, about 5 minutes. Scrape down sides of bowl. Add eggs, one at a time, ensuring each egg is fully incorporated prior to adding the next, 20 to 30 seconds each. Scrape down sides of bowl. Add mashed sweet potato and vanilla extract, beating until combined, 30 seconds to 1 minute. (The batter may break but will come back together soon.) Add flour mixture, and continue to beat until combined and smooth, about 1 minute. Scrape down sides of bowl. Contine to beat for 10 to 15 seconds. Fold in carrots. Divide batter among prepared pans.
8. Bake until a wooden pick inserted in center comes out clean, 25 to 30 minutes. Let cool in pans for 10 minutes. Remove from pans, and let cool completely on wire racks.
9. For the frosting: In the bowl of a stand mixer fitted with the paddle attachment, beat butter on medium speed until fluffy and lighter in color, about 2 minutes. Add cream cheese, and continue to beat until fluffy and combined, about 2 minutes. Add confectioners' sugar, meringue powder, vanilla extract, and salt, and continue to beat until combined and smooth, 2 to 3 minutes. Scrape down sides of bowl. Continue to beat for 30 seconds to 1 minute.
10. Place 1 cooled cake layer on a cake stand. Dollop with a generous amount of frosting, and spread evenly. Repeat with remaining 2 cake layers and frosting, and stack layers. Spread remaining frosting on top and sides of cake.

# sweet potato cupcakes
## WITH TOASTED MARSHMALLOW FROSTING

MAKES 12 CUPCAKES

*Enriched with spices that hint at classic holiday pies, these cupcakes are topped with a toasted meringue that mimics the beloved topping of traditional sweet potato casseroles. These cupcakes combine the best flavors of holiday baking into one tempting dessert.*

CUPCAKES:
- 1¾ cups (219 grams) all-purpose flour
- 2 teaspoons (4 grams) pumpkin pie spice
- 1 teaspoon (5 grams) baking powder
- 1 teaspoon (2 grams) ground cinnamon
- ½ teaspoon (2.5 grams) baking soda
- ½ teaspoon (1.5 grams) kosher salt
- 1 cup (220 grams) firmly packed light brown sugar
- 1 cup (244 grams) canned sweet potato purée
- ½ cup (100 grams) granulated sugar
- ½ cup (112 grams) vegetable oil
- 2 large eggs (100 grams), room temperature
- ¼ cup (60 grams) sour cream, room temperature
- 1 tablespoon (13 grams) vanilla extract

FROSTING:
- 1 tablespoon (15 grams) fresh lemon juice
- 1¼ cups (250 grams) granulated sugar
- 4 large egg whites (120 grams)
- 1 tablespoon (21 grams) corn syrup
- ½ teaspoon (1 gram) cream of tartar
- 2 teaspoons (8 grams) vanilla extract

**1.** Preheat oven to 350°F (180°C). Line a 12-cup muffin pan with paper liners.

**2.** For the cupcakes: In a large bowl, whisk together flour, pie spice, baking powder, cinnamon, baking soda, and salt.

**3.** In a medium bowl, whisk together brown sugar, sweet potato purée, granulated sugar, and oil until sugars dissolve, 2 to 3 minutes. Whisk in eggs, sour cream, and vanilla extract until fully combined. Fold in flour mixture until just combined. Divide batter among prepared muffin cups, filling each about three-fourths full.

**4.** Bake until a wooden pick inserted in center comes out clean, 20 to 22 minutes. Let cool in pan for 5 to 10 minutes. Remove from pan, and let cool completely on a wire rack.

**5.** For the frosting: In the bowl of a stand mixer, place lemon juice. Using a paper towel, wipe down sides and bottom of bowl with lemon juice until nothing remains. (This will help remove any oils and excess moisture from the bowl.) Let dry.

**6.** In the top of a double boiler, whisk together granulated sugar, egg whites, and corn syrup. Cook over simmering water, whisking frequently, until sugar fully dissolves and an instant-read thermometer registers 150°F (65°C). (Sugar is dissolved when you can rub the mixture between your fingers and feel no sugar.)

**7.** Transfer sugar mixture to the cleaned bowl of a stand mixer fitted with the whisk attachment. Add cream of tartar, and beat on low speed, increasing mixer speed to medium as mixture becomes bubbly. Beat until stiff peaks form and meringue is glossy and white, 7 to 10 minutes. Add vanilla, beating until fully combined, about 1 minute. Transfer to a 12-inch pastry bag fitted with your favorite piping tip. Pipe frosting on top of each cupcake. Using a handheld kitchen torch, carefully brown frosting.

# apple crisp blondies

MAKES 9 BLONDIES

*The rustic charm of an apple crisp and the chewy goodness of blondies combine in a symphony of fall flavors. Serve with a scoop of vanilla ice cream and drizzle with caramel for an exquisite dessert.*

**TOPPING:**
- ¾ cup (75 grams) old-fashioned oats
- ⅔ cup (83 grams) all-purpose flour
- ½ cup (110 grams) firmly packed light brown sugar
- 1 teaspoon (2 grams) ground cinnamon
- ½ teaspoon (1.5 grams) kosher salt
- ½ teaspoon (1 gram) ground nutmeg
- 7 tablespoons (98 grams) cold unsalted butter, cubed

**FILLING:**
- 2 small Gala apples (370 grams), cored and cubed
- ½ cup (110 grams) firmly packed light brown sugar
- 1 teaspoon (5 grams) fresh lemon juice
- 1 teaspoon (2 grams) ground cinnamon
- ½ teaspoon (1 gram) ground nutmeg
- Pinch kosher salt
- 1 tablespoon (14 grams) unsalted butter

**BLONDIES:**
- 1 cup (220 grams) firmly packed light brown sugar
- ½ cup (113 grams) unsalted butter, melted
- 1 large egg (50 grams), room temperature
- 1 teaspoon (4 grams) vanilla extract
- 1 cup (125 grams) all-purpose flour
- 1 teaspoon (2 grams) ground cinnamon
- ½ teaspoon (2.5 grams) baking powder
- ½ teaspoon (1.5 grams) kosher salt

Vanilla ice cream and Salted Caramel (recipe on page 29), to serve

**1.** Preheat oven to 350°F (180°C). Using a pastry brush, brush an 8-inch square baking pan with Cake Release (recipe on page 31) or spray with baking spray with flour. Line pan with parchment paper, letting excess extend by 1 inch over all sides of pan. (See note.)

**2.** For the topping: In a medium bowl, stir together oats, flour, brown sugar, cinnamon, salt, and nutmeg until well combined. Using your fingertips, cut in butter until pea-size crumbs remain. Cover and refrigerate until ready to use.

**3.** For the filling: In a large bowl, add apples, brown sugar, lemon juice, cinnamon, nutmeg, and salt. Toss to coat apples. Let stand until liquid forms, about 10 minutes.

**4.** In a medium skillet, melt butter over medium heat. Add apple mixture, and cook, stirring occasionally, until apples have softened and liquid thickens, 10 to 15 minutes. Remove from heat, and let cool.

**5.** For the blondies: In a medium bowl, whisk together brown sugar and melted butter until mixture appears creamy, about 2 minutes. Whisk in egg until well combined, about 1 minute. Whisk in vanilla extract until combined. Add flour, cinnamon, baking powder, and salt, and fold until a thick batter forms and flour is no longer visible, about 1 minute. Spread batter in prepared pan. Spoon filling on top. Sprinkle with topping.

**6.** Bake until edges are set and center is slightly jiggly, 50 to 55 minutes. Let cool for 1 hour. Serve with a scoop of ice cream, and drizzle with Salted Caramel.

**NOTE:** *It is mandatory to use parchment paper! These will stick otherwise.*

# cinnamon-apple-pecan bread

MAKES 1 (9X5-INCH) LOAF

*Each slice of this quick bread is packed with tender chunks of apple and crunchy pecans and infused with cinnamon and a touch of nutmeg. This delightful treat is ideal for breakfast, served with a smear of butter, or as a snack on a chilly afternoon.*

APPLES:
- 2 cups (200 grams) chopped Honeycrisp apples
- 3 tablespoons (36 grams) granulated sugar
- 1 teaspoon (4 grams) ground cinnamon

STREUSEL:
- ¼ cup (55 grams) firmly packed light brown sugar
- 2 tablespoons (28 grams) salted butter, melted
- ½ teaspoon (1 gram) ground cinnamon
- 6 tablespoons (48 grams) all-purpose flour
- 3 tablespoons (24 grams) chopped pecans
- Pinch kosher salt

BREAD:
- 2¼ cups (281 grams) all-purpose flour
- ½ cup (71 grams) chopped pecans
- 2 teaspoons (10 grams) baking powder
- 1 teaspoon (2 grams) ground cinnamon
- ½ teaspoon (1.5 grams) kosher salt
- ½ teaspoon (1 gram) ground nutmeg
- ¾ cup (170 grams) salted butter, room temperature
- ¾ cup (165 grams) firmly packed light brown sugar
- ½ cup (100 grams) granulated sugar
- 3 large eggs (150 grams), room temperature
- 1½ teaspoons (6 grams) vanilla extract
- ½ cup (120 grams) sour cream, room temperature

**1.** Preheat oven to 325°F (170°C). Spray a 9x5-inch loaf pan with baking spray with flour. Line pan with parchment paper, letting excess extend over long sides of pan. Place a sheet pan on bottom rack of oven. (This will help catch any streusel that falls over edges of the loaf pan.)

**2.** For the apples: In a medium bowl, toss together all ingredients.

**3.** For the streusel: In a medium bowl, stir together brown sugar, melted butter, and cinnamon. Add flour, pecans, and salt. Stir until crumbles form. Cover and refrigerate until ready to use.

**4.** For the bread: In a medium bowl, whisk together flour, pecans, baking powder, cinnamon, salt, and nutmeg.

**5.** In the bowl of a stand mixer fitted with the paddle attachment, beat butter, brown sugar, and granulated sugar on medium-low speed until fluffy and sugars dissolve, about 2 minutes, scraping down sides of bowl. Add eggs, one at a time, ensuring each egg is fully incorporated prior to adding the next, about 15 seconds each. Add vanilla extract, and continue to beat until combined. With mixer on medium-low speed, gradually add flour mixture alternately with sour cream and apples, beginning and ending with flour mixture, beating until just combined after each addition. Spoon into prepared pan. Top with streusel.

**6.** Bake until a wooden pick inserted in center comes out clean, 1 hour and 20 minutes to 1½ hours. Let cool in pan for 20 minutes. Using excess parchment as handles, remove from pan, and let cool completely on wire rack.

# browned butter-maple-pecan cookies

## MAKES ABOUT 15 COOKIES

*As you take your first bite, the soft and chewy textures of this cookie are coupled with the cozy warmth of cinnamon and the sweetness of maple. These cookies are one of my favorite treats to share with friends on crisp fall afternoons.*

| | |
|---|---|
| 2¼ | cups (281 grams) all-purpose flour |
| ½ | teaspoon (2.5 grams) baking soda |
| ½ | teaspoon (1.5 grams) kosher salt |
| 2 | teaspoons (4 grams) ground cinnamon, divided |
| 1 | cup (208 grams) Browned Butter (recipe on page 28), room temperature |
| 1 | cup (208 grams) firmly packed light brown sugar |
| ½ | cup (100 grams) plus 3 tablespoons (36 grams) granulated sugar, divided |
| 1 | large egg (50 grams), room temperature |
| 1 | large egg yolk (19 grams), room temperature |
| 3 | tablespoons (63 grams) maple syrup |
| 1½ | teaspoons (6 grams) maple extract |
| ½ | cup (57 grams) roughly chopped pecans |

1. Preheat oven to 350°F (180°C). Line 3 rimmed baking sheets with parchment paper.
2. In a large bowl, whisk together flour, baking soda, salt, and ½ teaspoon (1 gram) cinnamon.
3. In the bowl of a stand mixer fitted with the paddle attachment, beat Browned Butter, brown sugar, and 3 tablespoons (36 grams) granulated sugar at medium speed until light and fluffy, about 3 minutes, scraping down sides of bowl. Reduce mixer speed to medium-low. Add egg, egg yolk, maple syrup, and maple extract, and beat for 1 minute. Scrape down sides of bowl. Continue to beat for 2 minutes. Gradually add flour mixture, beating until just combined. Fold in pecans.
4. In a small bowl, whisk together remaining ½ cup (100 grams) granulated sugar and remaining 1½ teaspoons (3 grams) cinnamon.
5. Using a 3-tablespoon scoop, scoop dough, and roll each into a ball. Toss in cinnamon sugar. Place 2 inches apart on prepared pans (5 per pan).
6. Bake until edges are set and centers are puffy, 12 to 15 minutes. Let cool on pans for 5 minutes. Using a spatula, remove from pans, and let cool completely on wire racks.

# *pumpkin cinnamon rolls*

MAKES 12 ROLLS

*A lush browned butter cream cheese frosting drapes each roll in a tangy glaze, complementing the deep pumpkin flavors of the filling. What sets these rolls apart is the sugar cookie streusel topping that bakes into a crispy contrast to the fluffy dough beneath.*

**DOUGH:**
- ½ cup (120 grams) warm whole milk (105°F/41°C to 110°F/43°C)
- ½ cup (100 grams) plus 1 tablespoon (12 grams) granulated sugar
- 1 tablespoon (9 grams) active dry yeast
- ¾ cup (183 grams) canned pumpkin purée
- 1 large egg (50 grams), room temperature
- 4 cups (500 grams) all-purpose flour, plus more for dusting
- ½ cup (62 grams) cake flour
- 1 tablespoon (6 grams) ground cinnamon
- ½ teaspoon (1 gram) ground nutmeg
- ⅛ teaspoon ground cloves
- ¼ cup (57 grams) salted butter, room temperature

**TOPPING:**
- ⅔ cup (84 grams) all-purpose flour
- ½ cup (110 grams) firmly packed light brown sugar
- ¼ cup (57 grams) salted butter, room temperature
- ½ teaspoon (1 gram) ground cinnamon
- Pinch kosher salt (optional)

**FILLING:**
- ¾ cup (165 grams) firmly packed light brown sugar
- ½ cup (113 grams) unsalted butter, room temperature
- 2 tablespoons (32 grams) canned pumpkin purée
- 1 tablespoon (6 grams) ground cinnamon
- ½ teaspoon (1 gram) ground ginger
- ½ teaspoon (1 gram) ground nutmeg
- ¼ teaspoon ground cloves
- ½ cup (120 grams) heavy whipping cream

**GLAZE:**
- 4 ounces (113 grams) cream cheese, room temperature
- 2 cups (140 grams) confectioners' sugar
- 5 tablespoons (65 grams) Browned Butter (recipe on page 28), room temperature
- ½ teaspoon (1 gram) pumpkin pie spice

**1.** For the dough: In the bowl of a stand mixer, whisk together warm milk, 1 tablespoon (12 grams) granulated sugar, and yeast by hand. Let stand until bloomed and foaming, 5 to 10 minutes. Add pumpkin and egg, and whisk by hand until well combined. Add flours, cinnamon, nutmeg, cloves, and remaining ½ cup (100 grams) granulated sugar. Using your hands (or a silicone spatula), gently fold mixture until a shaggy dough forms.

**2.** Fit stand mixer with the dough hook attachment, and knead dough on medium speed until dough begins to smooth, 5 to 7 minutes. Add butter, 2 tablespoons (28 grams) at a time, kneading after each addition until no streaks of butter remain, about 45 seconds each. Continue to knead until dough is smooth and elastic, about 10 minutes. Stop mixer, and perform the windowpane test. (See Pro Tip on page 35.)

**3.** Place dough in a well-oiled bowl. Cover and let rise in a warm, draft-free place (75°F/24°C) until doubled in size, 1½ to 2 hours.

**4.** Preheat oven to 350°F (180°C). Line a rimmed baking sheet with parchment paper.

**5.** For the topping: In a small bowl, stir together flour, brown sugar, butter, cinnamon, and salt (if using) until crumbs form. Spread on prepared pan.

**6.** Bake until golden brown, 6 to 8 minutes. Let cool completely. Break into small pieces. Leave oven on.

**7.** For the filling: In a medium bowl, stir together all ingredients. (The mixture will look like it's split, but that's normal.)

**8.** Spray a 13x9-inch baking pan with cooking spray.

**9.** Lightly punch down dough. Turn out onto a well-floured surface, and roll into an 18x12-inch rectangle. Spread filling onto dough in an even layer, coating entire surface. Starting with one short side, roll dough into a log. Pinch flap of dough on each end to seal log. Using a serrated kitchen knife, slice log into 12 rolls. Place rolls, cut side up, in prepared pan. Cover and let rise in a warm, draft-free place (75°F/24°C) until puffed, 20 to 30 minutes.

**10.** Pour cream on top of and around rolls.

**11.** Bake until rolls are slightly golden brown, 25 to 30 minutes. Let cool in pan for 20 minutes.

**12.** For the glaze: In a medium bowl, beat cream cheese with a handheld mixer on medium speed until smooth, 1 to 2 minutes. Add confectioners' sugar, Browned Butter, and pie spice. Gradually increase mixer speed to medium, and beat until smooth, 1 to 2 minutes. Spread glaze onto rolls. Sprinkle topping onto glaze.

# candied sweet potato cobbler

MAKES 8 SERVINGS

*Tender sweet potato slices are bathed in a caramel sauce and infused with warming spices, creating an indulgent filling that is then topped with a perfectly crispy, golden-brown cobbler crust. This will be on my holiday table for years to come.*

FILLING:
- 2½ pounds (1,134 grams) sweet potatoes (about 3 large potatoes), peeled and sliced crosswise ¼ inch thick
- 1 cup (220 grams) firmly packed light brown sugar
- ½ cup (113 grams) unsalted butter, melted
- 1 tablespoon (6 grams) ground cinnamon
- 2 teaspoons (8 grams) vanilla extract
- ¾ teaspoon (2.25 grams) kosher salt
- ½ teaspoon (1 gram) ground nutmeg
- ½ teaspoon (1 gram) ground ginger

TOPPING:
- 2½ cups (313 grams) all-purpose flour, plus more for dusting
- ½ cup (100 grams) granulated sugar
- 1 tablespoon (15 grams) baking powder
- 2 teaspoons (4 grams) ground cinnamon
- 1 teaspoon (3 grams) kosher salt
- ¼ teaspoon (1.25 grams) baking soda
- ½ cup (113 grams) cold unsalted butter, cubed
- ⅓ cup (80 grams) cold whole buttermilk
- 2 teaspoons (8 grams) vanilla extract

Vanilla ice cream, to serve

1. Preheat oven to 375°F (190°C). Line a baking sheet with parchment paper.
2. For the filling: In 13x9-inch baking dish, place sweet potatoes.
3. In a small bowl, stir together brown sugar, melted butter, cinnamon, vanilla extract, salt, nutmeg, and ginger. Pour over sweet potatoes, tossing to ensuring all slices are coated.
4. Bake until bubbly and thickened, about 1 hour.
5. Meanwhile, for the topping: In a medium bowl, whisk together flour, granulated sugar, baking powder, cinnamon, salt, and baking soda until well combined. Add cold butter. Using your hands, cut butter into flour mixture until pea-size pieces remain. Add cold buttermilk and vanilla extract. Using a wooden spoon, stir until a shaggy dough forms.
6. Turn out dough onto a lightly floured surface. Gently pat crumbs into dough until no longer shaggy. Pat or roll dough into a 1-inch-thick rectangle. Using a sharp knife, cut into quarters. Stack quarters on top of each other, and pat down into 1-inch-thick rectangle. Repeat procedure 2 more times, making sure to press back into a 1-inch-thick rectangle each time. Using a rolling pin, roll dough to ½-inch thickness. Using a 2¾-inch round cutter, cut dough without twisting cutter. (Simply press into dough. Otherwise, the biscuits will not rise properly.) Place 1 inch apart on prepared pan. Fold any excess dough back together, and roll to ½-inch thickness. Cut dough, and place on prepared pan. Repeat until no dough remains. Refrigerate until ready to use, at least 30 minutes.
7. Remove sweet potato filling from oven. Place topping on filling.
8. Continue to bake until sweet potatoes are fork-tender and topping is golden brown, 20 to 22 minutes more. Let cool for 10 minutes. Serve with ice cream.

# sweet potato pie crème brûlées
**MAKES 6 CRÈME BRÛLÉES**

*Under a delicate layer of torched meringue and a sprinkle of crushed graham crackers waits a silky sweet potato custard infused with aromatic spices like cinnamon, nutmeg, and cloves.*

## CRÈME BRÛLÉES:

- 1 cup (244 grams) canned sweet potato purée
- 1¾ cups (420 grams) heavy whipping cream
- 1 teaspoon (2 grams) ground cinnamon
- 1 teaspoon (6 grams) vanilla bean paste
- ¼ teaspoon ground nutmeg
- Pinch kosher salt
- 5 large egg yolks (95 grams)
- ½ cup (100 grams) plus 6 teaspoons (24 grams) granulated sugar, divided

Boiling water

## MERINGUE:

- 1 tablespoon (15 grams) fresh lemon juice
- 3 large egg whites (90 grams), room temperature
- ½ cup (100 grams) granulated sugar
- ¼ teaspoon cream of tartar
- ½ teaspoon (2 grams) vanilla extract
- Pinch kosher salt

Garnish: crushed graham crackers

1. Preheat oven to 300°F (150°C).
2. On a paper towel-lined plate, spread sweet potato purée. Blot with additional paper towels. To ensure that the custard won't curdle from extra moisture, repeat until paper towels are no longer wet when pressed into purée. (I ended with about 60 grams purée.)
3. In a medium saucepan, heat cream, cinnamon, vanilla bean paste, nutmeg, and salt over low heat, stirring frequently, until warm, 5 to 7 minutes. (Do not boil.)
4. In a large bowl, whisk together egg yolks and ½ cup (100 grams) sugar until lightened in color, 2 to 3 minutes. Add blotted sweet potato purée. Whisk until smooth. Slowly add cream mixture, whisking constantly. Strain mixture through a fine-mesh sieve into a heatproof liquid-measuring cup to remove any air bubbles.
5. Place 6 (6-ounce) ramekins in a baking pan. Spoon ½ cup (109 grams) custard into each ramekin. Place pan in oven. Pour boiling water into baking pan until water covers the bottom one-fourth of ramekins.
6. Bake until edges are set but centers are still jiggly and an instant-read thermometer inserted in center registers 175°F (79°C), 30 to 40 minutes*. Carefully, transfer ramekins to a wire rack, and let cool for 1 hour. Refrigerate for at least 4 hours, ideally overnight, to set.
7. Just before serving, sprinkle remaining 6 teaspoons (24 grams) granulated sugar on top of custards. Using a handheld kitchen torch, carefully brown the sugar.
8. Meanwhile, for the meringue: In the bowl of a stand mixer, place lemon juice. Using a paper towel, wipe down sides and bottom of bowl with lemon juice until nothing remains. Let dry.
9. In the top of a double boiler, whisk together egg whites and granulated sugar. Cook over simmering water, whisking frequently, until sugar fully dissolves and an instant-read thermometer registers 150°F (65°C).
10. Transfer egg white mixture to the cleaned bowl of a stand mixer fitted with the whisk attachment. Add cream of tartar, and beat on low speed, increasing mixer speed to medium as mixture becomes bubbly. Beat until stiff peaks form and meringue is glossy and white, 7 to 10 minutes. Add vanilla extract, beating until fully combined. Transfer meringue to a 12-inch pastry bag fitted with your favorite piping tip. Pipe meringue on top of each custard. Using a handheld kitchen torch, carefully brown meringue. Garnish with graham crackers, if desired.

*If there is still liquid in the center, continue to bake for 5 to 10 minutes more.

# ginger-miso cookies

**MAKES 24 COOKIES**

*The miso imparts a subtle umami depth that enhances the cookie's buttery flavor, and bits of candied ginger sprinkled throughout provide a spicy kick that tingles the palate. This unique combination results in a chewy, flavorful cookie that surprises and satisfies with each bite!*

| | |
|---|---|
| 2¼ | cups (281 grams) all-purpose flour |
| 1½ | tablespoons (9 grams) ground ginger |
| 1 | teaspoon (5 grams) baking soda |
| ⅛ | teaspoon ground nutmeg |
| ¾ | cup (170 grams) unsalted butter, softened |
| 1½ | tablespoons (24 grams) white miso paste |
| 1 | cup (200 grams) granulated sugar |
| ¼ | cup (55 grams) firmly packed light brown sugar |
| 1 | large egg (50 grams), room temperature |
| 1 | large egg yolk (19 grams), room temperature |
| 2 | teaspoons (8 grams) vanilla extract |
| ½ | cup (80 grams) diced candied ginger, divided |

**1.** Preheat oven to 350°F (180°C). Line 4 baking sheets with parchment paper.

**2.** In a medium bowl, whisk together flour, ground ginger, baking soda, and nutmeg.

**3.** In the bowl of a stand mixer fitted with the paddle attachment, beat butter and miso paste on medium-low speed for 2 minutes. Add sugars, and continue to beat until fluffy and slightly lightened in color, about 3 minutes, scraping down sides of bowl. Add egg, egg yolk, and vanilla extract, beating until combined. Gradually add flour mixture, beating until fully incorporated, about 1 minute. Using a silicone spatula or large spoon, fold in half of candied ginger. Refrigerate for 10 minutes.

**4.** Scoop dough by 2 tablespoonfuls, and roll each into a ball. Press a few pieces of remaining candied ginger into each ball, and place 6 dough balls on each baking sheet.

**5.** Bake, one pan at a time, until centers are puffy and edges are set and just slightly golden brown, 11 to 12 minutes. Let cool on pan for 10 minutes. Remove from pan, and let cool completely on wire racks.

# salted caramel whoopie pies

**MAKES 22 WHOOPIE PIES**

*These whoopie pies are a delicious way to enjoy a cake and a cookie all in one. The tender cookies, with just a hint of vanilla, perfectly complements the sweet and salty caramel filling.*

COOKIES:
- 3 cups plus 2 tablespoons (391 grams) all-purpose flour
- 1 teaspoon (5 grams) baking powder
- ½ teaspoon (2.5 grams) baking soda
- ½ teaspoon (1.5 grams) kosher salt
- ½ teaspoon (1 gram) ground cinnamon
- ½ cup (113 grams) unsalted butter, room temperature
- 1 cup (200 grams) granulated sugar
- ¼ cup (55 grams) firmly packed light brown sugar
- 2 tablespoons (28 grams) vegetable oil
- 2 large eggs (100 grams), room temperature
- 1½ teaspoons (6 grams) vanilla extract
- 1 teaspoon (4 grams) butter emulsion (optional)
- ½ cup (120 grams) sour cream, room temperature
- ½ cup (120 grams) whole milk, room temperature

FILLING:
- 1 cup (227 grams) unsalted butter, room temperature
- 4 ounces (113 grams) cream cheese, room temperature
- 4 cups (480 grams) confectioners' sugar
- 1 to 2 tablespoons (15 to 30 grams) heavy whipping cream
- 2 teaspoons (20 grams) meringue powder
- 1 teaspoon (4 grams) vanilla extract
- ¼ teaspoon kosher salt

Salted Caramel (recipe on page 29)

1. Preheat oven to 350°F (180°C). Line baking sheets with parchment paper.
2. For the cookies: In a large bowl, whisk together flour, baking powder, baking soda, salt, and cinnamon.
3. In the bowl of a stand mixer fitted with the paddle attachment, beat butter, granulated sugar, brown sugar, and oil on medium speed until fluffy, about 3 minutes, scraping down sides of bowl halfway through mixing. Add eggs, one at a time, ensuring each egg is fully incorporated prior to adding the next, about 15 seconds each. Beat in vanilla extract and butter emulsion (if using) until combined.
4. In a small bowl, whisk together sour cream and milk. With mixer on low speed, add half of sour cream mixture to butter mixture, beating until combined. (Batter may split, but this is OK. It will come back together when the dry ingredients are added.) Beat in half of flour mixture until just combined. Repeat with remaining sour cream mixture and remaining flour mixture, scraping down sides of bowl and beating just until combined. Using a 2-tablespoon spring-loaded scoop, scoop dough (about 28 grams each), and place 2 inches apart on prepared pans.
5. Bake, one pan at a time, until edges are set and centers are puffy, 9 to 11 minutes. Let cool on pans for 5 minutes. Remove from pans, and let cool completely on a wire rack.
6. For the filling: In the bowl of a stand mixer fitted with the paddle attachment, beat butter on medium speed until smooth and fluffy, about 3 minutes. Add cream cheese, beating until well combined, about 1 minute. Add confectioners' sugar, cream, meringue powder, vanilla extract, and salt, and slowly increase mixer speed to medium, beating until well combined, 1 to 2 minutes. Beat on high speed until fluffy, about 20 seconds. Place buttercream in a pastry bag fitted with your favorite piping tip.
7. Pair up cookies so they are similar in shape and size. Pipe filling around outer edge of flat side of half of cookies. Fill centers with 2½ teaspoons (about 8 grams) Salted Caramel. Place remaining cookies, flat side down, on top to make a sandwich. Drizzle each whoopie pie with Salted Caramel as desired.

# no-bake sweet potato cheesecake

MAKES 1 (9-INCH) CHEESECAKE

*This cheesecake is a luscious delight that combines the warm, earthy tones of sweet potato with the velvety texture of cheesecake. Topped with a light, airy maple whipped cream, each bite is finished with a kiss of maple syrup!*

CRUST:
- 18 graham cracker sheets (270 grams)
- 3 tablespoons (36 grams) granulated sugar
- 1 teaspoon (2 grams) ground cinnamon
- ¼ teaspoon kosher salt
- 10 tablespoons (140 grams) unsalted butter, melted

FILLING:
- 3 (8-ounce) packages (680 grams) cream cheese, softened
- 1½ cups (180 grams) confectioners' sugar
- 1 tablespoon (13 grams) vanilla extract
- 2 teaspoons (8 grams) ground cinnamon
- ½ teaspoon (1 gram) ground ginger
- ½ teaspoon (1 gram) ground nutmeg
- ¼ teaspoon ground cloves
- Pinch kosher salt
- 1 cup (244 grams) canned sweet potato purée
- 1 cup (240 grams) cold heavy whipping cream

TOPPING:
- 1¼ cups (300 grams) cold heavy whipping cream
- 2 tablespoons (42 grams) maple syrup
- ½ teaspoon (2 grams) maple extract (optional)
- Pinch kosher salt

**1.** For the crust: In the work bowl of a food processor, process graham crackers, granulated sugar, cinnamon, and salt until uniform and fine. With processor running, add melted butter in a slow, steady stream until mixture begins to resemble wet sand. Using a silicone spatula, scrape down sides of bowl, and process for 15 to 20 seconds to ensure butter has fully coated the crumbs. Pour into a 9-inch springform pan. Using the bottom of a cup, press mixture into bottom and up sides of pan. Refrigerate until ready to use.

**2.** For the filling: In the bowl of a stand mixer fitted with the paddle attachment, beat cream cheese, confectioners' sugar, vanilla extract, cinnamon, ginger, nutmeg, cloves, and salt on low speed until combined, 1 to 2 minutes. Add sweet potato purée, and continue to beat until no visible streaks of sweet potato remain, 20 to 30 seconds, scraping down sides of bowl. Continue to beat until fully incorporated.

**3.** In a large bowl, beat cold cream with a handheld mixer on medium-high speed until stiff peaks form, 3 to 5 minutes. Using a silicone spatula, fold whipped cream into sweet potato mixture until smooth. Pour into prepared crust. Spread smooth. Refrigerate until set, at least 6 hours, ideally overnight.

**4.** For the topping: In a large bowl, beat cold cream with a handheld mixer on medium-high speed until stiff peaks form, 3 to 5 minutes. Add maple syrup, maple extract (if using), and salt, and continue to beat until just combined. (Be sure not to overmix or the cream will begin to separate!) Spoon topping onto cheesecake. Serve immediately.

# maple bacon macarons

MAKES ABOUT 20 MACARONS

*These macarons blend the sweet allure of maple with savory bacon. Featuring a smooth, glossy shell that gives way to a maple-infused buttercream and a piece of crispy bacon to surprise the palate, marrying the contrasting flavors into a harmonious delight.*

**MACARON SHELLS:**
- 1 tablespoon (15 grams) fresh lemon juice
- 2 cups (240 grams) confectioners' sugar
- 1¼ cups (120 grams) superfine almond flour
- ½ cup plus 1 tablespoon (120 grams) granulated sugar
- Scant 9 tablespoons (130 grams) egg whites (4 to 5 large egg whites)
- ½ teaspoon (1 gram) cream of tartar
- 1½ teaspoons (6 grams) maple extract
- 1 teaspoon (4 grams) vanilla extract

**FILLING:**
- 6 ounces (170 grams) cream cheese, room temperature
- 3 tablespoons (42 grams) unsalted butter, room temperature
- 3 cups (360 grams) confectioners' sugar
- 2 tablespoons (30 grams) heavy whipping cream
- 2 teaspoons (8 grams) maple extract
- ½ teaspoon (1 gram) ground cinnamon
- 6 slices applewood-smoked bacon (54 grams), cooked and crumbled

**1.** For the macaron shells: Line 3 rimmed baking sheets with a 2-inch macaron silicone baking mats.

**2.** In the bowl of a food processor, process confectioners' sugar and almond flour until well combined, about 30 seconds. Sift twice into a large bowl.

**3.** In the bowl of a stand mixer, place lemon juice. Using a paper towel, wipe down sides and bottom of bowl with lemon juice until nothing remains. (This will help remove any oils and excess moisture from the bowl.) Let dry.

**4.** In the top of a double boiler, whisk together granulated sugar, egg whites, and cream of tartar. Cook over simmering water, whisking frequently, until sugar fully dissolves and an instant-read thermometer registers 150°F (65°C).

**5.** Transfer egg white mixture to the cleaned bowl of a stand mixer fitted with the whisk attachment. Beat on low speed, increasing mixer speed to medium as mixture becomes bubbly. Beat until stiff peaks form and meringue is glossy and white, 7 to 10 minutes. Add extracts, beating until just combined.

**6.** Using a silicone spatula, gradually fold in flour mixture until fully combined. Continue folding until batter is smooth and flows like lava. The batter is ready once you can move the spatula over the batter in a figure eight motion and the batter does not break.

**7.** Transfer batter to a pastry bag fitted with a ½-inch round piping tip. Holding piping tip perpendicularly to a prepared pan, pipe batter onto circles on silicone mat. Firmly tap pans vigorously on counter 5 to 7 times to release air bubbles. Repeat with remaining batter on remaining pans. If any bubbles do not pop, use a wooden pick to pop bubbles. Let stand at room temperature until a skin forms and they are no longer shiny, 35 minutes to 45 minutes. (This process may take longer if your home is more humid.)

**8.** Preheat oven to 300°F (150°C).

**9.** Bake, one pan at a time, until macaron shells form a bubbly bottom edge, 16 to 18 minutes. (When touched, the macaron shells should not move around.) Let cool completely on pans.

**10.** For the filling: In the bowl of a stand mixer fitted with the paddle attachment, beat cream cheese and butter on medium speed until smooth, 1 to 2 minutes. Add confectioners' sugar, cream, maple extract, and cinnamon, and continue to beat until combined, about 1 minute.

**11.** Transfer filling to a pastry bag fitted with your favorite piping tip. Pipe a border onto flat side of half of macaron shells. Place ½ teaspoon bacon in center of each border. Place remaining macaron shells, flat side down, on top, pressing slightly. Dab the top of each macaron with filling. Sprinkle with bacon.

# chocolate heaven

# classic chocolate chip cookies

**MAKES 17 COOKIES**

*I am such a purist when it comes to my chocolate chip cookies. They need a ton of chocolate chips, a strong vanilla and brown sugar flavor, and, most importantly, crispy edges and chewy, soft centers. So, I stopped searching for the perfect CCC at bakeries and made it in my own kitchen.*

| | |
|---|---|
| 2¾ | cups (344 grams) all-purpose flour |
| ¾ | teaspoon (3.75 grams) baking powder |
| ½ | teaspoon (2.5 grams) baking soda |
| ½ | teaspoon (1.5 grams) kosher salt |
| 3.5 | ounces (99 grams) quality dark chocolate, chopped |
| 1½ | cups (384 grams) mini semisweet chocolate chips |
| 1 | cup (255 grams) milk chocolate chips |
| 1 | cup (227 grams) salted butter, room temperature |
| ¾ | cup (150 grams) granulated sugar |
| ¾ | cup (165 grams) firmly packed light brown sugar |
| 1 | large egg (50 grams), room temperature |
| 1 | large egg yolk (19 grams), room temperature |
| 1 | tablespoon (13 grams) vanilla extract |

Flaked sea salt, to taste

1. Line a baking sheet with parchment paper.
2. In a large bowl, whisk together flour, baking powder, baking soda, and kosher salt.
3. In a medium bowl, stir together chocolates.
4. In the bowl of a stand mixer fitted with the paddle attachment, beat butter and sugars on medium-low speed until light and fluffy, 3 to 4 minutes, scraping down sides of bowl. Add egg, egg yolk, and vanilla extract; continue to beat until all ingredients are well combined, about 1 minute. Reduce to low, and then gradually add flour mixture to butter mixture, beating until just combined. Beat in half of chocolate mixture.
5. Using a 3-tablespoon spring-loaded cookie scoop, scoop dough, and roll in remaining chocolate mixture to coat. Firmly press chocolate into dough. Place on prepared pan. (They can be touching.) Cover, and refrigerate for 20 minutes.
6. Preheat the oven to 325°F (170°C). Line baking sheets with parchment paper.
7. Working in batches, place 5 dough balls 2 to 3 inches apart on prepared pans.
8. Bake, one pan at a time, until centers are puffy and edges are set, 15 to 18 minutes. To ensure the perfect circular cookie, place the open end of a large cup around edges of each cookie, swirling cup in a circular motion, making sure to touch edges with each movement. Let cool for 10 minutes. Sprinkle with sea salt to taste.

**NOTE:** *I love chocolate chip cookies loaded with chocolate chips. If you prefer less, feel free to cut the chocolate chips in half.*

# *campfire pie*

MAKES 1 (9½-INCH) PIE

*This pie captures the indescribable feeling of sitting around a campfire on a cool summer night. It's a buttery graham cracker crust with a brownie base, Nutella layer on top, and a charred meringue top to give you nothing but pure nostalgia in every bite.*

CRUST:
- 18 graham cracker sheets (270 grams)
- 2 tablespoons (24 grams) granulated sugar
- ½ cup (113 grams) salted butter, melted

FILLING:
- 5.2 ounces (150 grams) quality dark chocolate, chopped
- ¼ cup (57 grams) unsalted butter
- ¼ cup (56 grams) vegetable oil
- ¾ cup (150 grams) granulated sugar
- ½ cup (110 grams) firmly packed light brown sugar
- 1 cup (125 grams) all-purpose flour
- ⅓ cup (28 grams) unsweetened cocoa powder
- ½ teaspoon (1.5 grams) kosher salt
- ¼ teaspoon (1.25 grams) baking soda
- 3 large eggs (150 grams), room temperature and lightly beaten
- 2 teaspoons (8 grams) vanilla extract
- ½ cup (128 grams) chocolate-hazelnut spread*

TOPPING:
- 1 tablespoon (15 grams) fresh lemon juice
- 5 large egg whites (150 grams)
- 1⅓ cups (267 grams) granulated sugar
- 1 teaspoon (4 grams) vanilla extract

1. Preheat oven to 350°F (180°C).
2. For the crust: In the work bowl of a food processor, process graham crackers and granulated sugar until fine crumbs form. With processor running, slowly add melted butter. Scrape down sides of bowl. Continue to process until texture resembles wet sand. Using the bottom of a cup, press mixture into bottom and up sides of a 9½-inch round tart pan with removable bottom.
3. Bake until golden brown and set, 10 to 12 minutes. Leave oven on.
4. For the filling: In the top of a double boiler, combine chocolate, butter, and oil. Cook over simmering water, stirring occasionally, until chocolate and butter are melted and mixture is smooth. Turn off heat, and whisk in granulated sugar and brown sugar until well combined. Remove from heat, and let cool slightly, 3 to 5 minutes.
5. In a medium bowl, whisk together flour, cocoa powder, salt, and baking soda.
6. Slowly add beaten eggs to melted chocolate mixture, whisking until combined. Whisk in vanilla. Fold in flour mixture until just combined. Pour mixture into prepared crust.
7. Bake until a wooden pick inserted in center comes out with a few moist crumbs, 35 to 40 minutes. Let cool in pan for 1 hour.
8. In a small microwave-safe bowl, microwave chocolate-hazelnut spread until spreadable, 10 to 20 seconds. Spread on top of pie.
9. For the topping: In the bowl of a stand mixer, place lemon juice. Using a paper towel, wipe down sides and bottom of bowl with lemon juice until nothing remains. (This will help remove any oils and excess moisture from the bowl.) Let dry.
10. In the top of a double boiler, whisk together egg whites and granulated sugar. Cook over simmering water, whisking frequently, until sugar fully dissolves and an instant-read thermometer registers 150°F (65°C). (Sugar is dissolved when you can rub the mixture between your fingers and feel no sugar.)
11. Transfer egg white mixture to the cleaned bowl of a stand mixer fitted with the whisk attachment. Beat on low speed, increasing mixer speed to medium as mixture becomes bubbly. Beat until stiff peaks form and meringue is glossy and white, 7 to 10 minutes. Add vanilla extract, and continue to beat until just combined. Spread on top of chocolate-hazelnut layer. Using a handheld kitchen torch, carefully brown topping.

*I use Nutella.*

# edible cookie dough bars

**MAKES 10 BARS**

*Sometimes you don't feel like baking, but you want something fun to snack on. Let your kids join you in the kitchen to help make these, or make them all by yourself and stash the rest in the freezer for a secret treat after the kids are in bed. No worries—I won't tell!*

DOUGH:
- 1¾ cups (219 grams) cake flour
- ½ cup (113 grams) salted butter, room temperature
- ¾ cup (90 grams) confectioners' sugar
- ½ cup (110 grams) firmly packed light brown sugar
- 3 tablespoons (45 grams) heavy whipping cream, room temperature
- 2 teaspoons (8 grams) vanilla extract
- ¼ teaspoon kosher salt
- 1 cup (224 grams) mini semisweet chocolate chips

COATING:
- 1 cup (170 grams) chopped semisweet chocolate
- 1 tablespoon (14 grams) coconut oil

Flaked sea salt, to taste

**1.** Preheat oven to 350°F (180°C).

**2.** For the dough: On a rimmed baking sheet, spread flour.

**3.** Bake for 5 to 7 minutes, checking every 2 minutes for any signs of burning. Let cool completely on pan.

**4.** In a large bowl, beat butter, confectioners' sugar, and brown sugar with a handheld mixer on medium speed until fluffy, about 2 minutes, scraping down sides of bowl. Add cream, vanilla, and kosher salt, and continue to beat until combined. Gradually add cooled flour, folding with a silicone spatula. Fold in chocolate chips. Spoon batter into 10 wells of a 2x1-inch bar silicone mold. Refrigerate for at least 1 hour to set.

**5.** For the coating: In the top of a double boiler, combine chocolate and oil. Cook over simmering water, stirring occasionally, until chocolate and oil are melted and mixture is smooth.

**6.** Remove cookie dough bars from molds, and dip each into coating, letting excess drip off. Let stand on a wire rack until set. Sprinkle with sea salt to taste.

# million dollar cake

MAKES 1 (9-INCH) CAKE

*Too often, white chocolate doesn't get the love it deserves, so I made this cake to really showcase its decadent beauty. The cake is slightly fudgy, with a white chocolate and vanilla bean base. Brushed with edible gold, this cake is bougie, and I love it dearly.*

- 2¼ cups (450 grams) granulated sugar
- 1½ cups (360 grams) whole milk
- 1¼ cups (284 grams) salted butter
- 8 ounces (226 grams) quality white chocolate, chopped
- 3 large eggs (150 grams), room temperature
- 2 teaspoons (12 grams) vanilla bean paste
- 2 cups (250 grams) all-purpose flour
- 1½ cups (188 grams) cake flour
- 1 teaspoon (5 grams) baking powder
- ½ teaspoon (1.5 grams) kosher salt
- 3 cups (600 grams) Swiss Meringue Buttercream (recipe on page 27)

Garnish: edible gold leaf

1. Preheat oven to 325°F (170°C). Using a pastry brush, brush a tall-sided 9-inch round cake pan with Cake Release (recipe on page 31) or spray with baking spray with flour.

2. In a medium saucepan, heat sugar, milk, and butter over medium-low heat, whisking frequently, until butter is melted, about 5 minutes. Add white chocolate. Cook, stirring constantly, until white chocolate is fully melted, 3 to 5 minutes. Remove from heat. Let cool for 10 minutes. Add eggs and vanilla bean paste. Whisk until fully combined, 2 to 3 minutes.

3. In a large bowl, whisk together flours, baking powder, and salt. Using a silicone spatula, fold in sugar mixture until just combined. (Batter may appear lumpy, but that's OK! It comes out perfect every time.) Pour batter into prepared pan.

4. Bake until a wooden pick inserted in center comes out clean, 1 hour and 40 minutes to 1 hour and 50 minutes. Let cool in pan for 15 minutes. Remove from pan, and let cool completely on a wire rack.

5. Spread Swiss Meringue Buttercream on top of cooled cake as desired. Brush gold leaf on top of frosting, if desired.

# no worries chocolate cake

**MAKES 1 (13X9-INCH) CAKE**

*In college, one of my friends broke up with her boyfriend, broke her foot, and found out she flunked an exam all in the same day. So, what did I do to console her? I grabbed a bottle of cheap wine and made this cake. It's a beautifully smooth chocolate cake with a chocolate-hazelnut frosting on top. When you take a bite, all your worries will go away.*

CAKE:
- ¾ cup (180 grams) sour cream, room temperature
- 3 large eggs (150 grams), room temperature
- 1½ teaspoons (6 grams) vanilla extract
- 1 cup (240 grams) warm whole milk, (105°F/41°C to 110°F/43°C)
- 1 teaspoon (2 grams) espresso powder
- 2 cups (250 grams) all-purpose flour
- 1½ cups (300 grams) granulated sugar
- 1 cup (85 grams) unsweetened cocoa powder
- ¾ cup (165 grams) firmly packed light brown sugar
- ½ cup plus 2 tablespoons (140 grams) unsalted butter, cubed and room temperature
- ½ cup (112 grams) vegetable oil
- 2 tablespoons (10 grams) black cocoa powder
- 2 teaspoons (10 grams) baking powder
- 1 teaspoon (3 grams) kosher salt
- ½ teaspoon (2.5 grams) baking soda

FROSTING:
- 1 cup (227 grams) unsalted butter, softened
- 4 ounces (113 grams) cream cheese, softened
- 4 cups (480 grams) confectioners' sugar
- 1 cup (256 grams) chocolate-hazelnut spread*
- 2 tablespoons (10 grams) unsweetened cocoa powder
- 5 tablespoons (75 grams) heavy whipping cream
- 2 teaspoons (12 grams) vanilla extract

Garnish: shaved milk chocolate

1. Preheat oven to 350°F (180°C). Using a pastry brush, brush a 13x9-inch baking dish with Cake Release (recipe on page 31) or spray with baking spray with flour.
2. For the cake: In a medium bowl, whisk together sour cream, eggs, and vanilla extract.
3. In a small bowl, stir together hot milk and espresso powder.
4. In the bowl of a stand mixer fitted with the paddle attachment, beat flour, granulated sugar, unsweetened cocoa powder, brown sugar, butter, oil, black cocoa powder, baking powder, salt, and baking soda on medium-low speed until mixture has a sandy texture and butter is fully incorporated. Add sour cream mixture, and continue to beat until smooth. Scrape down sides of bowl. Continue to beat until well combined. Add hot milk mixture; continue to beat until well combined. Pour batter into prepared pan.
5. Bake until a wooden pick inserted in center of cake comes out clean, 35 to 40 minutes. Let cool in pan for 5 minutes. Remove from pan, and let cool completely on a wire rack.
6. For the frosting: In the bowl of a stand mixer fitted with the paddle attachment, beat butter on medium-low speed until creamy, about 2 minutes. Add cream cheese; continue to beat until well combined, 30 seconds to 1 minute. Add confectioners' sugar, chocolate-hazelnut spread, and cocoa powder. Gradually increase mixer speed to medium. Add cream, 1 tablespoon (15 grams) at a time, beating until well combined. Add vanilla extract, and continue to beat until well combined and smooth. Spread on top of cooled cake. Garnish with chocolate, if desired.

*I use Nutella.

"*a party without a cake is just a meeting.*"

— JULIA CHILDS

# chocolate-hazelnut-stuffed chocolate chip cookies

MAKES 14 COOKIES

*Picture sinking your teeth into warm, gooey chocolate chip cookies, only to discover a pocket of chocolate-hazelnut spread hidden inside. These cookies are truly unforgettable.*

| | |
|---|---|
| 11 | tablespoons (176 grams) chocolate-hazelnut spread* |
| 1½ | cups (190 grams) bread flour |
| 1¼ | cups (156 grams) cake flour |
| 1 | teaspoon (5 grams) baking soda |
| ¾ | teaspoon (2.25 grams) kosher salt |
| ½ | cup (113 grams) salted butter, room temperature |
| ½ | cup (96 grams) all-vegetable shortening |
| 1 | cup (220 grams) firmly packed light brown sugar |
| ½ | cup (100 grams) granulated sugar |
| 1 | large egg (50 grams), room temperature |
| 1 | large egg yolk (19 grams), room temperature |
| 1 | tablespoon (18 grams) vanilla extract |
| 7 | ounces (200 grams) quality dark chocolate, roughly chopped and divided |

Flaked sea salt, to taste

**1.** Spoon chocolate-hazelnut spread onto a parchment paper-lined baking sheet in 1-tablespoon mounds. Flatten into disks. Freeze until set, at least 30 minutes.

**2.** Preheat oven to 350°F (180°C). Line several baking sheets with parchment paper.

**3.** In a large bowl, whisk together flours, baking soda, and kosher salt.

**4.** In the bowl of a stand mixer fitted with the paddle attachment, beat butter and shortening on medium-low speed until creamy, about 1 minute. Add sugars, and continue to beat until sugars dissolve and mixture is light and fluffy, about 3 minutes. Add egg, egg yolk, and vanilla extract; continue to beat until just combined, about 1 minute. Scrape down sides and bottom of bowl. Reduce mixer speed to low, and gradually add flour mixture, beating until just combined. Using a silicone spatula, fold in half of chocolate (100 grams).

**5.** Using a ¼-cup spring-loaded cookie scoop, scoop dough, and roll into balls. Using your fingers, press an indentation into center of each ball, and place a frozen chocolate-hazelnut spread disk into indentation. Roll dough into balls, ensuring disks are covered completely. Press 3 to 4 pieces of remaining chocolate into dough. Place 3 dough balls 2 to 3 inches apart on each prepared pan.

**6.** Bake, one pan at a time, until edges are set and centers are puffy, 13 to 16 minutes. To ensure the perfect circular cookie, place the open end of a large cup around edges of each cookie, swirling cup in a circular motion, making sure to touch edges with each movement. Let cool for 10 minutes. Sprinkle with sea salt to taste. Remove from pans, and let cool completely on wire racks.

*\*I use Nutella.*

# midnight cheesecake-topped brownies

MAKES 8 BROWNIES

*This dessert is the ultimate treat for any chocolate lover. Every mouthwatering forkful is the perfect balance of heavenly cheesecake and exquisite chocolate.*

BROWNIES:
- 4.4 ounces (124 grams) quality dark chocolate, chopped
- ¼ cup (57 grams) salted butter
- ¼ cup (56 gram) vegetable oil
- ¾ cup (150 grams) granulated sugar
- ½ cup (110 grams) firmly packed light brown sugar
- ¾ cup (94 grams) all-purpose flour
- ½ cup (43 grams) unsweetened cocoa powder
- ½ teaspoon (1.5 grams) kosher salt
- ⅛ teaspoon baking soda
- 3 large eggs (150 grams), room temperature and lightly beaten
- 2 teaspoons (8 grams) vanilla extract
- 4.4 ounces (124 grams) quality milk chocolate, chopped

TOPPING:
- 5 cream-filled chocolate sandwich cookies* (67 grams)
- 1 (8-ounce) package (226 grams) cold cream cheese
- ¾ cup (90 grams) confectioners' sugar
- 1 teaspoon (4 grams) vanilla extract
- Pinch kosher salt
- ½ cup (120 grams) cold heavy whipping cream

Garnish: broken cream-filled chocolate sandwich cookies*

1. Preheat oven to 350°F (180°C). Line an 8-inch round cake pan with parchment paper.
2. For the brownies: In the top of a double boiler, combine dark chocolate, butter, and oil. Cook over simmering water, stirring occasionally, until chocolate and butter are melted and mixture is smooth. Turn off heat, and whisk in granulated sugar and brown sugar until well combined. Remove from heat, and let cool slightly, 3 to 5 minutes.
3. In a medium bowl, whisk together flour, cocoa powder, salt, and baking soda.
4. Slowly add eggs to melted chocolate mixture, whisking until combined. Whisk in vanilla extract. Fold in flour mixture until just combined. Carefully fold in milk chocolate until evenly distributed. Pour mixture into prepared pan.
5. Bake until a wooden pick inserted in center comes out with a few moist crumbs, 35 to 40 minutes. Let cool in pan on wire rack for 1 hour.
6. For the topping: In the work bowl of a food processor, pulse cookies until small, uniform crumbs form.
7. In the bowl of a stand mixer fitted with the paddle attachment, beat cold cream cheese at medium speed until smooth, 1 to 2 minutes. Add confectioners' sugar, vanilla extract, and salt, and continue to beat until combined.
8. Switch to the whisk attachment. Add cold cream, and beat at medium speed until fully incorporated and mixture is fluffy, 2 to 3 minutes. Add cookie crumbs, and continue to beat until just combined.
9. Transfer topping to a pastry bag fitted with your favorite piping tip. Pipe topping onto brownies, or simply spread topping onto brownies in an even layer. Garnish with broken cookies, if desired.

*I use Oreos.

# the best brownies ever.
## PERIOD.

**MAKES 9 BROWNIES**

*This is one of my favorite recipes in the WORLD. These brownies are super chocolaty and gooey. With pockets of milk chocolate in every bite, they literally melt in your mouth.*

| | |
|---|---|
| 4.4 | ounces (124 grams) quality dark chocolate, chopped |
| ¼ | cup (57 grams) unsalted butter, melted |
| ¼ | cup (56 grams) vegetable oil |
| ¾ | cup (150 grams) granulated sugar |
| ½ | cup (110 grams) firmly packed light brown sugar |
| ¾ | cup (94 grams) all-purpose flour |
| ½ | cup (43 grams) unsweetened cocoa powder |
| ½ | teaspoon (1.5 grams) kosher salt |
| ⅛ | teaspoon baking soda |
| 3 | large eggs (150 grams), room temperature and lightly beaten |
| 2 | teaspoons (8 grams) vanilla extract |
| 4.4 | ounces (124 grams) quality milk chocolate, chopped |

**1.** Preheat oven to 325°F (170°C). Line an 8-inch square baking pan with parchment paper, letting excess extend over sides of pan.

**2.** In the top of a double boiler, combine dark chocolate, butter, and oil. Cook over simmering water, stirring occasionally, until chocolate and butter are melted and mixture is smooth. Turn off heat, and whisk in sugars until well combined. Remove from heat, and let cool slightly, 3 to 5 minutes.

**3.** In a medium bowl, whisk together flour, cocoa powder, salt, and baking soda.

**4.** Slowly add eggs to chocolate mixture, whisking until combined. Whisk in vanilla extract. Fold in flour mixture until just combined. Carefully fold in milk chocolate until evenly distributed. Spread batter into prepared pan.

**5.** Bake until a wooden pick inserted in center comes out with a few moist crumbs, 30 to 35 minutes. Let cool in pan for 15 minutes. Using excess parchment as handles, remove from pan, and let cool completely on wire rack. To serve, cut into bars.

# the cookies that broke my diet

### MAKES ABOUT 8 LARGE COOKIES

*Do you know how hard it is to run a food blog and keep a well-balanced diet? I was doing well for about five days on some diet where it felt like I could only eat lettuce and almonds. Friday night hits, and I was violently craving a cookie. I went into the pantry, grabbed every salty and sweet item I could find, and smooshed them all into one giant cookie. These cookies broke my diet to smithereens. A chocolate chip cookie is loaded with salty crinkle chips, pecans, chocolate sandwich cookies, and pretzels and then dizzled with caramel. I hope these cookies won't break your diet, but if they do, you won't regret a single calorie.*

- 2¾ cups (344 grams) all-purpose flour
- 1 teaspoon (5 grams) baking soda
- ½ teaspoon (1.5 grams) kosher salt
- 1 cup (113 grams) pecan halves
- 1 cup (180 grams) mini semisweet chocolate chips
- 1 cup (45 grams) pretzels, roughly chopped
- 1 cup (30 grams) crinkle-cut potato chips, roughly chopped
- 10 cream-filled chocolate sandwich cookies (113 grams), roughly chopped
- 1 cup (227 grams) salted butter, room temperature
- ¾ cup (150 grams) granulated sugar
- ¾ cup (165 grams) firmly packed light brown sugar
- 1 large egg (50 grams), room temperature
- 1 large egg yolk (19 grams), room temperature
- 1 teaspoon (4 grams) vanilla extract

Flaked sea salt, to taste
Salted Caramel (recipe on page 29)

1. Preheat oven to 350°F (180°C). Line 3 baking sheets with parchment paper.
2. In a large bowl, whisk together flour, baking soda, and kosher salt.
3. In a medium bowl, stir together pecan halves, chocolate chips, pretzels, chips, and cookies.
4. In the bowl of a stand mixer fitted with the paddle attachment, beat butter on medium-low speed until creamy, about 2 minutes. Add sugars, and continue to beat until light and fluffy, about 3 minutes, scraping down sides of bowl. Add egg and egg yolk, and continue to beat until well combined. Beat in vanilla extract until well combined, about 1 minute. Gradually add flour mixture, beating until just combined. Add pecan mixture. Gradually increase mixer speed to medium-low, and beat until just combined, 20 to 30 seconds. Using a ½-cup measuring cup, scoop dough (about 130 grams each), and roll into balls, pressing tops slightly to flatten. Place 2 to 3 inches apart on prepared pans (3 per pan).
5. Bake until edges are set and centers are puffed, 13 to 16 minutes. Let cool on pans for 5 minutes. Remove from pans, and let cool completely on a wire rack. Sprinkle with sea salt to taste. Drizzle Salted Caramel onto cooled cookies.

# triple-chocolate cake

**MAKES 1 (8½X4½-INCH) CAKE**

*Chocolate on chocolate on chocolate? This one is for my chocolate lovers! Because there is never too much chocolate in one dessert, a plush sour cream chocolate loaf cake is topped with ganache and chocolate chips. It will be love at first bite.*

Cake:
- 1 cup (220 grams) firmly packed light brown sugar
- ½ cup (113 grams) salted butter, melted and slightly cooled
- ¼ cup (50 grams) granulated sugar
- 3 large eggs (150 grams), room temperature
- 1 large egg yolk (19 grams), room temperature
- 3 tablespoons (42 grams) vegetable oil
- 1 teaspoon (4 grams) vanilla extract
- ¾ cup (64 grams) unsweetened cocoa powder
- ½ cup (48 grams) almond flour
- 2 teaspoons (10 grams) baking powder
- 1½ teaspoons (2 grams) espresso powder
- ½ teaspoon (1.5 grams) kosher salt
- ¾ cup (180 grams) whole buttermilk, room temperature
- 1 cup (125 grams) all-purpose flour
- ¼ teaspoon (1.25 grams) baking soda

TOPPING:
- 6 tablespoons (90 grams) heavy whipping cream
- 4 ounces (113 grams) semisweet chocolate, chopped
- 1 tablespoon (21 grams) corn syrup

Garnish: semisweet chocolate chips

1. Preheat oven to 325°F (170°C). Line an 8½x4½-inch loaf pan with parchment paper, letting excess extend about 1 inch over sides of pan.
2. For the cake: In a large bowl, whisk together brown sugar, melted butter, granulated sugar, eggs, egg yolk, oil, and vanilla extract until sugars dissolve and fats are fully incorporated, about 2 minutes. Add cocoa powder, almond flour, baking powder, espresso powder, and salt, whisking until smooth. Add buttermilk, whisking until fully combined. Add all-purpose flour and baking soda, whisking until fully combined. Pour into prepared pan.
3. Bake until a wooden pick inserted in center comes out with a few moist crumbs, 1 hour to 1 hour and 10 minutes. Let cool in pan for 10 minutes. Remove from pan, and let cool completely on a wire rack.
4. For the topping: In a medium microwave-safe bowl, microwave cream on high for 1 minute. Add chocolate and corn syrup. Gently whisk until chocolate is melted. (If the chocolate isn't fully melted, microwave in 10- to 15-second intervals, whisking between each.)
5. Spread topping onto cooled cake. Garnish with chocolate chips, if desired.

# white chocolate-pistachio cheesecake

MAKES 1 (9-INCH) CHEESECAKE

*A white chocolate cheesecake is adorned with a vibrant pistachio layer, creating the most beautiful flavor combination known to man. To make it even better, it is topped with whipped cream and a generous sprinkling of pistachios.*

CRUST:
- 18 graham cracker sheets (270 grams)
- ¼ cup (50 grams) granulated sugar
- ¼ teaspoon kosher salt
- 10 tablespoons (140 grams) unsalted butter, melted

FILLING:
- 6 ounces (170 grams) quality white chocolate, chopped
- 1 cup (240 grams) heavy whipping cream, divided
- 4 (8-ounce) packages (904 grams) cream cheese, room temperature
- 1½ cups (180 grams) confectioners' sugar
- 1 tablespoon (12 grams) vanilla extract
- 1½ teaspoons (6 grams) pistachio emulsion
- 3 to 4 drops green gel food coloring

TOPPING:
- 1 cup (240 grams) heavy whipping cream
- ¼ cup (30 grams) confectioners' sugar
- 1 teaspoon (4 grams) vanilla extract
- Pinch kosher salt

Garnish: chopped toasted salted pistachios

**1.** Spray a 9-inch springform pan with cooking spray.

**2.** For the crust: In the bowl of a food processor, process graham crackers, granulated sugar, and salt until fine, uniform crumbs form. With food processor running, add melted butter. Stop and scrape down sides of bowl. Continue to process until texture resembles wet sand, about 1 minute. Using the bottom of a cup, press graham cracker mixture into bottom and up sides of prepared pan. Refrigerate until set, about 20 minutes.

**3.** For the filling: In a microwave-safe bowl, microwave white chocolate and ¼ cup (60 grams) cream on high for 1 minute; whisk. Microwave in 15-second intervals, whisking between each, until white chocolate is fully melted and mixture is combined. Refrigerate until cooled and thickened, 20 to 30 minutes.

**4.** In the bowl of a stand mixer fitted with the paddle attachment, beat cream cheese and confectioners' sugar on medium speed until fluffy and smooth, about 2 minutes. Beat in vanilla extract until combined. Refrigerate until chilled, 20 to 30 minutes.

**5.** In a large bowl, beat remaining ¾ cup (180 grams) cream with a handheld mixer at medium-high speed until stiff peaks form. Fold whipped cream into cream cheese mixture. Transfer 1½ cups cream mixture to a medium bowl.

**6.** Fold white chocolate ganache into remaining cream mixture in stand mixer bowl. Spoon into crust.

**7.** Fold pistachio emulsion and green food coloring into reserved cream mixture. Spoon mixture on top of white chocolate filling. Refrigerate until set, at least 4 hours, ideally overnight.

**8.** For the topping: In a large bowl, beat cream and confectioners' sugar with a handheld mixer on high speed until stiff peaks form. Fold in vanilla extract and salt. Spoon topping onto cheesecake, and sprinkle pistachios on top.

# caramelized white chocolate tiramisù

**MAKES 12 SERVINGS**

*Picture a classic tiramisù elevated to new heights with the addition of caramelized white chocolate, infusing a tantalizing depth of flavor to the traditional marscapone filling.*

- 12 ounces (340 grams) white chocolate, roughly chopped
- 3 cups (720 grams) heavy whipping cream
- 1 (8-ounce) container (226 grams) mascarpone cheese
- 2 teaspoons (12 grams) vanilla bean paste
- Pinch kosher salt
- Pinch ground nutmeg
- 2 cups (480 grams) brewed espresso
- 1 cup (240 grams) hazelnut or coffee liqueur
- 30 to 40 ladyfingers (225 to 300 grams)
- 2 tablespoons (10 grams) unsweetened cocoa powder

**1.** Preheat oven to 250°F (130°C).

**2.** On a rimmed baking sheet, place white chocolate.

**3.** Bake until melted, about 10 minutes. Using a silicone spatula, spread melted white chocolate on baking sheet, going back and forth, until it's as smooth as possible. Bake for 10 minutes more. Smooth white chocolate. Repeat procedure until white chocolate turns the color of butterscotch, 3 to 4 times. (The chocolate may become chalky but will become creamy again when you use the spatula to smooth it.)

**4.** In a large saucepan, heat cream, mascarpone, vanilla bean paste, salt, and nutmeg over medium-low heat, about 5 minutes, stirring until combined. Add caramelized white chocolate, scraping as much as possible off pan. Gently whisk until chocolate is fully incorporated and melted into cream mixture. Pour into a large bowl, and cover with plastic wrap. Refrigerate for at least 6 hours, ideally overnight.

**5.** In the bowl of a stand mixer fitted with the whisk attachment, beat cold white chocolate mixture on medium speed until thick and fluffy and stiff peaks form, 3 to 5 minutes. (Do not overmix! As soon as stiff peaks form, stop the mixer.)

**6.** In a small bowl, stir together espresso and liqueur.

**7.** Spread a layer of white chocolate mixture (about 1½ cups or 250 grams) into bottom of a 13x9-inch baking dish.

**8.** Quickly dip ladyfingers, one at a time, into espresso mixture, and place in a single layer on white chocolate mixture in pan, fitting as many as possible without overlapping. Spread half of remaining white chocolate mixture on top of ladyfingers in pan. Repeat layers with remaining ladyfingers and remaining white chocolate mixture. Refrigerate for at least 4 hours. Sift cocoa on top before serving.

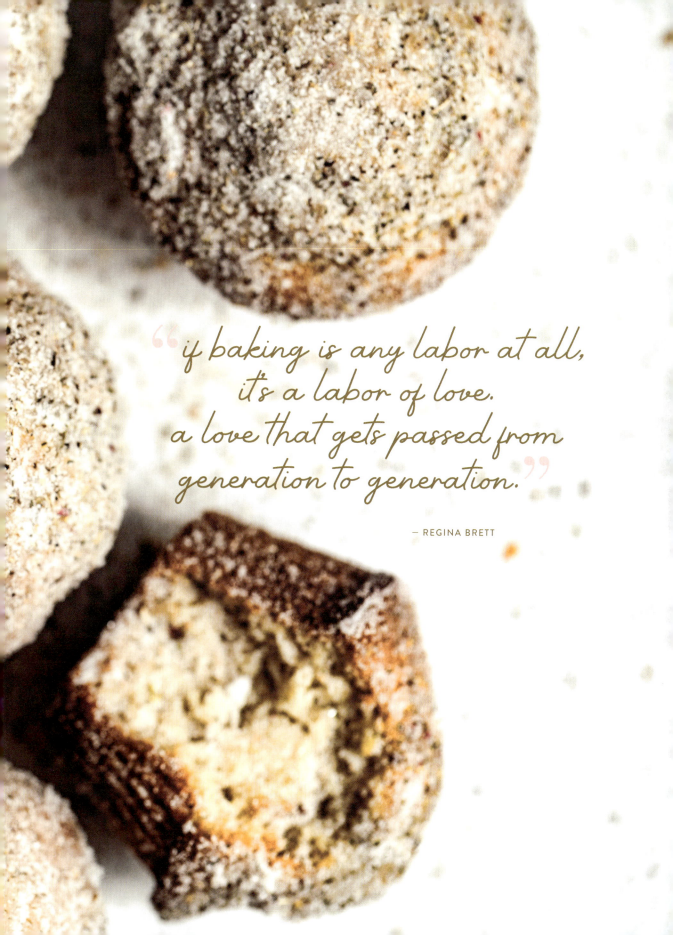

"*if baking is any labor at all, it's a labor of love. a love that gets passed from generation to generation.*"

— REGINA BRETT

# recipe index

### BARS, BLONDIES, AND BROWNIES
Apple Crisp Blondies, 204
The Best Brownies Ever. Period., 242
Cranberry Bars with Orange Shortbread Crust, 165
Edible Cookie Dough Bars, 231
Midnight Cheesecake-Topped Brownies, 241
Rowan's Lemon-Blueberry Bars, 180

### BASICS
Browned Butter, 28
Cake Release, 31
Pastry Cream, 30
Banana Milk Alternative, 30
Salted Caramel, 29
Swiss Meringue Buttercream, 27

### BISCUITS AND SCONES
Buttery Maple Biscuits, 60
Caramelized Onion, Bacon, and Gorgonzola Biscuits, 108
Homemade Buttermilk Biscuits, 104
Jalapeño, Corn, and Oaxaca Scones, 112
Milk Chocolate-and-Hazelnut Scones, 134

### BREADS, SAVORY
Asiago-and-Thyme Cheese Puffs, 95
Black Pepper-and-Gruyère Popovers, 99
Browned Butter Pecan Parker House Rolls, 103
Classic Dinner Rolls, 111
The Cornbread That Everyone Asks Me to Make Over and Over Again, 190
Croissant Loaf, 106
Fig, Proscuitto, Rosemary, and Olive Focaccia, 96

### BREADS, SWEET
Almond Croissant Loaf, 123
Apple Cider Doughnut Bars, 194
Banana Rum Cream Brioche Doughnuts, 34
Blueberry Pancake Muffins, 36
Café au Lait Beignets, 44
Chamomile Sugar Muffins, 42
Cinnamon-Apple-Pecan Bread, 206
Classic Banana Bread, 52
Mocha Swirl Buns with Coffee Cream Cheese Glaze, 40
Pumpkin Bread with Cinnamon Streusel and Buttery Maple Glaze, 196
Pumpkin Cinnamon Rolls, 210
Sage Browned Butter Doughnuts, 148
Sticky Bun Babka, 136
The Ultimate Cinnamon Rolls, 50

### CAKES
Aunt Hazel's Citrus Pound Cake, 163
Blood Orange Loaf Cake, 72
Chai Swiss Roll with Browned Butter-Cream Cheese Frosting, 54
Cherry-Almond Cake, 120
Churro Bundt Cake, 198
Classic Vanilla Pound Cake, 183
Coconut Cake with Passion Fruit Curd, 91
Coconut Cornbread Cake with Lime Frosting, 85
Double-Glazed Almond Pound Cake, 124
Earl Grey Cake with Citrus-Almond Buttercream, 58
Fresh Peach Olive Oil Cake, 86
Glazed Coconut Financiers, 56
Lemon-Raspberry Swiss Roll, 76
Million Dollar Cake, 232
Mom's Lemon Cake, 170
No Worries Chocolate Cake, 234
Salted Caramel Banana Cake with Cream Cheese Frosting, 67
Sweet Potato-Carrot Cake, 200
Triple-Chocolate Cake, 246
Wake-Me-Up Cappuccino Cake, 38

### CHEESECAKES
Ashley's Vanilla Bean Cheesecake, 188
Jayna's Snickerdoodle Cheesecake with Cookie Whipped Cream, 178
No-Bake Sweet Potato Cheesecake, 220
White Chocolate-Pistachio Cheesecake, 249

### COBBLERS AND CRISPS
Apple Bliss Crisp, 64
Berrylicious Four-Berry Crisp, 80
Candied Sweet Potato Cobbler, 212
Cardamom and Walnut Pear Crisp, 116
More-Crust-Than-Peaches Peach Cobbler, 70

### COOKIES
Bobbie's Fave Sugar Cookies, 166
Browned Butter-Maple-Pecan Cookies, 208
Candied Grapefruit Macarons, 88
Chocolate-Hazelnut–Stuffed Chocolate Chip Cookies, 238
Classic Chocolate Chip Cookies, 226
The Cookies That Broke My Diet, 245
Dad's White Chocolate Macadamia Nut Cookies, 173
Ginger-Miso Cookies, 216
Lavender Meringue Cookies, 145
Lemon-and-Fennel Shortbread Cookies, 142
Maple Bacon Macarons, 222
Matcha-and-Almond Sablés with White Chocolate Drizzle, 129
Peach Cobbler Whoopie Pies, 78
Pistachio-and-Apricot Sandwich Cookies, 130
Pistachio Sugar Cookies, 133
Sage, Browned Butter, and Parmesan Biscotti, 100
Salted Caramel Whoopie Pies, 218

### CRÈME BRÛLÉES
Orange Blossom Crème Brûlées, 154
Pomegranate Crème Brûlées, 68
Sweet Potato Pie Crème Brûlées, 214

### CUPCAKES
Ardyn's Cotton Candy Cupcakes, 169
Baklava-Stuffed Cupcakes with CInnamon-Orange Buttercream, 118
Butter Pecan Cupcakes, 126
Lavender Cupcakes with Lime Swiss Meringue Buttercream, 140
Rose Cupcakes with Champagne Frosting, 146
Sweet Potato Cupcakes with Toasted Marshmallow Frosting, 202

### LAYERED DESSERTS
Banana Pudding Pavlova, 82
Caramelized White Chocolate Tiramisù, 250
Lemon-Basil Trifles, 153
Mom's Midnight Cookie Crunch, 176
Strawberry-Lavender Eton Mess, 157

### PASTRIES
Hubby's Giant Blueberry Breakfast Pastry, 174
Rose Sugar Churros, 158
Salted Honey Mille-Feuilles, 187

### PIES AND TARTS
Campfire Pie, 228
Chocolate Tart with Espresso Whipped Cream, 46
Mile-High Cherry Meringue Tart, 74
Sweet Potato Pie, 184